INDICATORS OF
TERRORISM VULNERABILITY IN AFRICA

I. Introduction

1.1 Background Motivation

In 2006, David Kilcullen stated that there has been more written about insurgency in the last four years then the last four decades, when the terminology was created [2]. Terrorist organizations, in recent history, have been conducting operations similar to insurgents, such as living among the population in highly urbanized areas, where they conduct both recruiting and operations. It is important to note that this increased interest in terrorism is not based upon a single event, but in an increasing trend in terrorist attacks. From the years 1968-1997, the global average number of attacks ranged between 243 and 305 events annually. However, since 1997, that number has increased more than 6 times resulting in between 1589 to 1895 events per year [3]. Between these time periods, the lethality of terrorist attacks have also increased [3]. The United States government states that it has "no greater responsibility then ensuring the safety and security of the American people." [4] Today, the global terrorism threat presents the greatest viable threat to the American people and therefore, is one of the main focuses of the United States government, as well as the rest of the world.

Despite the importance of the issue, little is known about modern terrorism. Partially, this is due to the nature of today's insurgents, who differ significantly in terms of "policy, strategy, operational art, and tactical technique" from past insurgents [2].

1

Consequently, this puts the United States and the world as a whole in a position where we know little about this global threat. Furthermore, this lack of understanding of this adversary has caused the U.S. to take a reactionary stance to countering terrorism, instead of a preventative stance.

1.2 African Focus

Many individuals have analyzed relationships between variables at the country level and the number of terrorist attacks in that country. This analysis ranges in size from a global scale to southeastern Turkey. Despite this wide range, looking specifically at terrorism at the country level in Africa has not been conducted in the current literature.

Many terrorist groups have been both forming and/or expanding operations in Africa [5]. Additionally, Africa serves as both a recruiting ground and sanctuary for terrorists [6]. Africa creates a security dilemma for the United States. The advent of terrorism has caused the United States to be as vulnerable to weak states as strong states and the U.S. has a lot of poorly secured targets in Africa [6]. Consequently, American involvement has increased in Africa and the military established the AFRICOM command in February 2007 [6].

This provides a vast security dilemma for both Africa and the rest of the world. By focusing this research on Africa, specific insights into this problem can be gained, which can lead to a specific strategy to potentially prevent terrorist attacks in the future.

Africa has numerous traits that when aggregated drastically separate it from the rest of the world. Some of these traits include a low openness to trade, low primary school enrollment, a low investment portion of Gross Domestic Product (GDP), a high public spending portion of GDP, high population growth, and strategic resources such as oil and natural gas [5]. Consequently, this research focuses on Africa to unveil the specific relationships between socio-economic traits and the prevalence of vulnerability to terrorist attacks.

1.3 Problem Statement

To better understand the current terrorism threat in Africa, this research addresses the following three questions.

1. Can the qualitative relationships considered indicators of terrorism be quantitatively supported with a generalized linear model?

2. Can other potential indicators of terrorism be quantitatively explored and supported with a generalized linear model?

3. Can these variable relationships undergo classification methods, such as classification trees, in order to determine breakpoints in characteristics of countries, which indicate increased vulnerability to terror attacks?

Answering these questions helps confirm and/or explore which characteristics best describe patterns among terrorism targets in Africa. Then, determining breakpoints of these characteristics provides an opportunity to reduce Africa's vulnerability to terrorism. Terrorism reductions will occur by adopting a strategy that shapes the environment and limits specific areas of vulnerability from future terrorist attacks. The hope is these insights will be adopted by the U.S. to strategically disrupt the terrorism threat in Africa.

1.4 Proposed Approach

Multivariate techniques are applied to data characterizing each country, such as socio-economic and demographic attributes. The response variable is the annual number of terrorist attacks in an African country, while the independent variables are various socio-economic and other country characteristics. This analysis provides insight into African terrorism and helps suggest methods the U.S. can alter its strategy based upon this new information.

1.5 Preview

Chapter 2 discusses the compiled literature review associated with this problem. This includes important definitions, the current U.S. policy for counter-terrorism and similar research. This past research analyzes both common methodology techniques, as well as current beliefs about socio-economic statistics and terrorism. Chapter 3 focuses upon the methodology and analysis of the first research question listed in Section 1.3. This includes a description of the data, the proposed approach and accompanying assumptions, the analysis results, as well as the validation techniques. Chapter 4 focuses upon the methodology and analysis of the second research question listed in Section 1.3. This includes an overview of the data and results of the analysis. Chapter 5 further explores classification analysis for the indicators specified in Chapter 4 in order to find break-points in the data, which answers the third question listed in Section 1.3. Finally, Chapter 6 concludes the research, highlighting the research insights and detailing areas for future study.

II. Literature Review

This chapter begins by defining terms used throughout the research, then the current U.S. counter-terrorism policy is overviewed including homeland risk, and lastly, similiar research and their results are reviewed.

2.1 Definitions

Two important definitions to define upfront are terrorism and vulnerability.

Terrorism.

One commonly debated definition is that of terrorism. The Department of State defines terrorism as "means premeditated, politically motivated violence perpetrated against noncombatant targets by subnational groups or clandestine agents [7]." While the Department of Defense (DoD) defines terrorism as "The unlawful use of violence or threat of violence to instill fear and coerce governments or societies. Terrorism is often motivated by religious, political, or other ideological beliefs and committed in the pursuit of goals that are usually political [8]." Despite some similarities, even departments within the U.S. government do not use a consistent definition. For instance, the Department of State specifies that terrorist attacks are committed by subnational groups or agents against noncombatants, while the DoD does not include these specifications. While the differences may seem trivial at first, this means that the DoD could consider an attack from a nation against the U.S. military as a terrorist attack. Additionally, the Department of State clarifies that the terrorist attack must actually occur, while the DoD considers threats of terrorism as terrorist attacks. Therefore, the specific definition of terrorism used helps clearly define the scope of the analysis and to have clear boundaries defining what does and does not constitute an attack.

Enders and Sandler define terrorism as "the premeditated use or threat to use violence by individuals or subnational groups in order to obtain a political or social objective through the intimidation of a large audience beyond that of the immediate victims [9]." They go on to state that the majority of modern terrorism definitions have two main components, presence or threat of violence and political or social objective. Definitions also commonly explain that terrorism is committed by a perpetrator, against a victim, and for an audience. The Department of State and Department of Defense both contain these common components.

These common components of definitions of modern terrorism highlight much about modern terrorist. For instance, the goal of modern terrorism is to circumvent the standard politics of a country and cause political change through threats and violence [9]. Secondly, although attacks are premeditated and planned against certain targets, there is a secondary target, which is the audience. In order to instill fear in this audience, and therefore have some level of control over them, terrorists attempt to make their actions appear random. By doing this, the audience is unsure when or where the next attack will occur. Therefore, more fear is instilled in the audience because of the uncertainty around becoming victims of the next attack [9]. This leaves the population, or its representative government, with two distinct choices, concede to the terrorists or stop the terrorists. The U.S. has clearly stated its intention to stop terrorists [4], and must create an effective strategy to complete this task. Over the last decade, a strategy has been developed, but it has proven to be rather ineffective [10]. A new strategy must be adopted that will allow the U.S. to meet its goals.

The definition of terrorism used for this research is that used by the National Consortium for the Study of Terrorism and Responses to Terrorism (START). START uses the following definition to determine inclusion into the Global Terrorism Database

(GTD). The GTD defines a terrorist attack as "the threatened or actual use of illegal force and violence by a non-state actor to attain a political, economic, religious, or social goal through fear, coercion, or intimidation." For the database, to include an incident, all three of the following attributes must be present [11]:

1. The incident must be intentional, the result of a conscious calculation on the part of a perpetrator.

2. The incident must entail some level of violence or threat of violence including property violence, as well as violence against people.

3. The perpetrators of the incidents must be subnational actors. The database does not include acts of state terrorism.

Furthermore, at least two of the following three criteria must be present for an incident to be included into the GTD [11]:

Criterion 1: The act must be aimed at attaining a political, economic, religious, or social goal. In terms of economic goals, the exclusive pursuit of profit does not satisfy this criterion. It must involve the pursuit of more profound, systemic economic change.

Criterion 2: There must be evidence of an intention to coerce, intimidate, or convey some other message to a larger audience (or audiences) than the immediate victims. It is the act taken as a totality that is considered, irrespective if every individual involved in carrying out the act was aware of this intention. As long as any of the planners or decision makers behind the attack intended to coerce, intimidate or publicize, the intentionality criterion is met.

Criterion 3: The action must be outside the context of legitimate warfare activities. That is, the act must be outside the parameters permitted by international humanitarian law (particularly the prohibition against deliberately targeting civilians or non-combatants).

Vulnerability.

Haimes defines vulnerability as, "manifestation of the inherent states of the system that can be exploited to adversely affect that system." [12] This definition focuses on vulnerability from a systems perspective, which is useful for determining the different components of terrorism production. However, the DoD outlines the following definitions of vulnerability in DoD Instruction 2000.16: [13].

- In anti-terrorism, a situation or circumstance, which if left unchanged, may result in the loss of life or damage to mission essential resources.

- The susceptibility of a nation or military force to any action by any means through which its war fighting potential or combat effectiveness may be reduced or will to fight diminished.

- The characteristics of a system that cause it to suffer a definite degradation (incapability to perform the designated mission) as a result of having been subjected to a certain level of effects in an unnatural (man-made) hostile environment.

- The characteristics of an installation, system, asset, application, or its dependencies that could cause it to suffer a degradation or loss (incapacity to perform its designated function) as a result of having been subjected to a certain level of threat or hazard.

It is rather apparent, that the DoD definitions encompass Haimes definition for vulnerability and is specific to anti-terrorism. Consequently, the DoD definition of vulnerability is utilized throughout the remainder of the research.

2.2 Current Policy

It is vital to understand what is currently perceived about terrorism and the current U.S. policy regarding modern terrorism and its accompanying threats. This process begins with what the United States government is currently doing and the anti-terrorism National Security Strategies. The United States government's goal in regards to terrorism, especially al-Qa'ida is to "disrupt, degrade, dismantle and defeat" [4].

The plan of attack to achieve this goal is split into long term and short term strategies. The long term strategy is "advancing freedom and human dignity through effective democracy" [14]. The strategy uses democracy as a vessel for freedom and human dignity and is directly related to four aspects of the United States' beliefs about terrorism. First, the U.S. believes terrorists derive from political alienation within their own country. Democracy should aid this issue since every person has an equal role in the government. Second, terrorist beliefs grow out of past grievances with the government or other parties. Democracy settles disputes peacefully and orderly within the legal system. Third, terrorists come from conspiracy and misinformation subcultures and it is believed that freedom of speech allows them to hear the truth as well as the misinformation giving the individual more choices. Fourth, terrorists have an ideology that justifies murder. However, a respect for human dignity limits a mind set like this from ever taking place [14].

The U.S. government also specifically states some attributes which are believed not to promote terrorism. First, terrorism is not a result from a poverty mentality, which

9

is supposedly based upon the information the U.S. currently has about terrorists. Second, terrorism does not come from hostility to past U.S. policy, since the U.S. is not the only target. Third, terrorists are not motivated by U.S.-Israeli relations, because attacks were planned during the peace of the 1990's. Lastly, terrorism is not a response to U.S. offenses since we did not attack first [14].

The U.S. government's short term strategy is broken into four sub-strategies [14]:

Strategy 1. Preventing attacks from terrorists by preemptively attacking their resources, including leadership.

Strategy 2. Protecting the homeland by preventing entry of terrorists to the country and defending likely targets in the country.

Strategy 3. Denying terrorists access to weapons of mass destruction.

Strategy 4. Deny terrorists control of any country and eliminate terrorist safe havens.

There are two defined tactics to obtain these four sub-strategies. First, depriving non-state actors of funding, recruitment, information, and support (FRIS) [15]. Second, the United States focuses on defending itself. Clearly, the short term sub-strategies are basic defensive and offensive strategies of war and do not incorporate any specific tactics related to terrorism.

To accomplish these terrorism goals, the United States will need to reconsider strategy and incorporate all elements of its power, not only military elements. These measures are commonly divided into four groups, diplomatic, information, military, and economic (DIME model). The affect of the instruments of power are measured by the impact to political, military, economic, social, information, and infrastructure effects (PMESII) [15]. A major issue with these tools and effects are that they are complex, have unpredictable effects and interactions, and have no way to measure return on investment [15].

2.3 Homeland Risk

The Department of Homeland Security (DHS) is one organization that the U.S uses outside of military force to engage in counter-terrorism. DHS was created with the mission of "preventing terrorist attacks, reducing vulnerability to such attacks, and providing emergency response in the event of an attack." [16] The DHS strives to use risk assessment in order to better defend the nation through prevention and reduced vulnerability. Risk is commonly defined by the risk triplet: scenario, the probability of that scenario, and the consequences of that scenario [17].

Conducting a risk assessment of terrorism of this manner is an extremely difficult task. First, simply defining a scenario is extremely difficult, because terrorists will conduct any scenario that will meet their goals. To defend in this manner, one needs an exhaustive list of scenarios [18]. With the enemy being able to make decisions and able to react to any defensive move that the United States implements, creating an exhaustive list of scenarios would be essentially impossible. For an exercise in scope, the DHS was asked to compile a list of "critical assets" to defend the dispersion of its budget to certain areas. The list had 77,069 entries [16]. Next, every potential scenario would have to be applied to these "critical assets." This task would be endless if the scope were expanded to all possible targets.

The second portion of risk is calculating the probability of the scenario. Clearly, this is problematic, since few successful attacks have been conducted in the U.S. making scenario-specific probabilities difficult to calculate. Additionally, determining the probability of a scenario is extremely difficult due to the terrorist's ability to react, the defenses that the United States puts in place, and factors outside of both parties' control. Another suggestion is to replace the second portion of the risk triplet with a degree of difficulty to successfully accomplish the scenario against the target under consideration [19]. This degree of difficulty must take into account both terrorist

11

beliefs and homeland defense for a defined scenario [19]. As mentioned above, this is extremely difficult, but is much easier to calculate from the available data than a probability of scenario [19].

The last portion of the risk triplet is determining the consequences, which also requires a specified scenario and complex computations to compile accurate effects. Additionally, computing accurate effects is exceptional difficult due to second, and tertiary effects aside from the main effects. While fruitful attempts have been made to quantify the risks of terrorism, the task is very difficult to put a quantitative formula to human driven activities [20]. Risk analysis through these means is primarily focused upon the consequences and the mitigation of these consequences instead of the prevention of the attack.

Not only is the current counter-terrorism strategy at its core reactionary, it also lacks effectiveness. A survey paper [10] dedicated to evaluating current counter terrorism strategies came to the following conclusions. Despite billions of dollars spent annually on counter-terrorism strategies, very little research has been conducted to determine the effectiveness of these strategies. However, using the current available research, no counter-terrorism strategy consistently reduces the number of terrorist attacks. Using metal detectors caused a decreased number of skyjackings, but caused an increased number of non-skyjacking terrorist attacks. Clearly, metal detectors did not reduce the number of attacks, but instead displaced certain types of attacks. In risk analysis, this displacement is known as risk transference and implies that no risk is actually reduced. Additionally, fortifying embassies, protecting diplomats, higher punishments for skyjacking, and United Nation resolutions all showed no effect on the number of terrorist attacks. Furthermore, retaliation for terrorist attacks with military force, raised the number of attacks, especially in the short term. Lastly, having political parties that are intolerant of terrorist attacks increased the number of all types of terrorist attacks except for non-casualty attacks. The U.S. drastically needs to change counter-terrorism tactics in order to be more effective, and this needs to come from a better understanding of terrorism.

The DHS has made preliminary moves to better understand terrorist and have decided to analyze simple risk indicators beyond the already described event-based models for risk assessment [16]. These risk indicators do not use the current knowledge of terrorist preferences and priorities to help prioritize targets to defend, but are an attempt to look at the general types of targets that terrorists attack. The first metric is the product of population and population density [16]. This shows that terrorists prefer to target large population centers, which is concurrent with other research stating that terrorist attacks are positively correlated with population [21, 22]. This makes sense since terrorists aim to influence a population based upon fear and more people will be fearful since more people will experience an attack and the media is more likely to report a large attack. It is additionally interesting to note that modern terrorists conceal themselves in cities and industrialized centers rather than rural areas. Historically, insurgents would hide in rural areas away from people that are able to detect them. However, changes in technology has made hiding in cities more effective, especially when blending in with a sympathetic population. Additionally, it puts insurgents right next to the individuals they are trying to "win" [2].

Another indicator that the DHS uses is the product of population, population density, and sum of critical infrastructure elements [16]. It is not surprising that terrorists are going to additionally focus on critical infrastructure elements, since this increases the amount of people impacted by the attack, as well as the affect of the attack itself. These indicators take the terrorist strategy into account and allows the United States to better protect itself and are the beginning of a good defensive strategy. However, since there are many population centers and critical infrastructure elements, more indicators should be identified in order to develop better defenses and even more indicators are necessary to create a preventative strategy or predictive model.

2.4 Similar Research

In the academic community, many scholars have attempted to determine relationships between certain socio-economic country characteristics and terrorism, specifically where terrorists originate or target. Despite the amount of research, many socio-economic characteristics remain unexplored or highly debated. In order to learn from this previous research and understand current knowledge in the academic community, similar academic research has been analyzed and summarized to include common methodologies and current relationship beliefs about certain socio-economic country characteristics and terrorist attacks.

Prominent Variable Relationships.

Carter's Five Factors.

Terrorism has become a topic of study for many institutions, including those outside of the military and government. Interest has come from individuals in psychology, sociology, economics, medical and engineering studies.

One approach to determine the kind of factors that contribute to a terrorist mindset or make countries vulnerable to a terrorist mindset is to analyze countries that currently provide safe haven for terrorist networks or at least allow them to operate unabated. Carter [23] analyzed countries which harbor, willingly or unwillingly, terrorist networks in the Middle East and the Horn of Africa. Carter qualitatively assessed these countries to have five factors in common. These factors included poverty, lack of border control, political corruption, fragile economies, and social fragmentation [23]. It is important to note that these factors were not quantitatively assessed, but rather based upon observation. However, each variable intuitively makes sense to have a relationship with the number of terrorist attacks in a country and worthwhile for further analysis.

The first factor is poverty. The aim of terrorism is to use fear to coerce the population into joining and supporting their cause. Poverty allows terrorism to operate on many levels. First, impoverished countries usually have impoverished governments that are unable to provide the necessary services to deter terrorism. Second, impoverished countries have impoverished people that are more vulnerable to being recruited by terrorist. Insurgents are no longer seeking money, but actually have financial power to "win" the population [2].

The U.S. government agrees with the belief that terrorism is related to poverty [4, 14]. However, the quantitative literature on the relationship between economics and terrorists attacks, tell a much different story. GDP per capita and number of terrorist attacks have shown to have a negative relationship in some quantitative research based upon the belief that it is cheaper to attack impoverished people [21], while other research shows a significant positive relationship based upon the belief that terrorist want to target wealthier people, since more people will become aware of the attack [24]. Additionally, other research has analyzed the non-linear terms as well and shown that the relationship between GDP per capita and number of terrorist attacks is actually a concave parabolic function as shown in Figure 1 [25, 22, 26]. One reason for the difference in findings could be related to the difference in methodologies. Li [21], which found a negative relationship, using a pooled time series approach, while Street [24] came to the opposite conclusion with a Poisson panel estimation based upon analyzing an attacks by where the home nation of the attackers, instead of the actual location of the attack. However, this parabolic finding could further explain the differing results. The parabolic finding is further supported by three different researchers with two different methodologies, zero-infalted negative binomial regression [25, 26] and Poisson regression [22, 26], coming to the same conclusion.

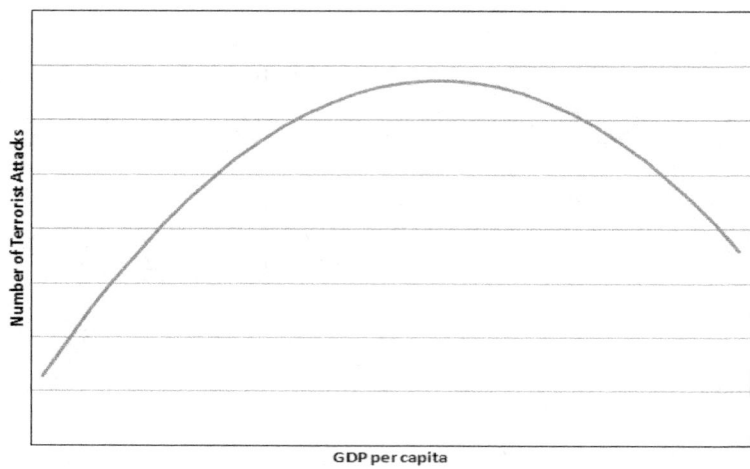

Figure 1. Notionalized relationship between the number of terrorist attacks and GDP per capita

Another method to evaluate poverty is based upon income inequality. This approach is based upon the belief that poverty is relative, individuals only feel impoverished in comparison to wealthy neighbors. Consequently, income inequality is another interesting factor for analysis and has shown a positive relationship to the number of terrorist attacks using a pooled time series approach [21].

The second factor is lack of border control. A country lacking border control is related to a country lacking security means. A lack of border control provides terrorists the means to easily and safely transport supplies, finances, and people, making attacks easier and survival possible. A simple increase in border control could be useful in inhibiting terrorists and increasing the cost of conducting attacks. While there is little literature showing statistical quantitative support for border security, Piazza [27] indicates strength of government as an important factor. From a failed state perspective, the strength of the government is negatively correlated with number

16

of terrorist attacks based upon a negative binomial regression model.

The third factor is political corruption. Once again, [27] Piazza shows a negative relationship exists between corrupt governments and security necessary to prevent terrorism. Additionally, a corrupt government does not have the support of its people and the people do not feel like the government will protect them when necessary. This relationship has some statistical support when analyzing from the failed state perspective using negative binomial regression.

The fourth factor is fragile economies, which is related to poverty. However, the fragility of the economy also makes the country more vulnerable to terrorist attacks, since an attack will be so devastating that the country will have difficulty "bouncing back" causing the effect of the attack to be much greater. Additionally, joining a terrorist network could be the only form of a steady income for a family.

A direct measure of economic fragility is difficult to obtain. Proxies for the fragility of economies could include the interaction with other economies or the globalization of a nation. Conducting a pooled time series analysis, the interaction with other economies and globalization were both shown to have a positive relationship with the number of terrorist attacks [21]. However, analyzing non-linear terms showed a convex parabolic relationship between international trade and the number of attacks as seen in Figure 2 [25], it is important to note that this article focused on the nationalities of people attacked instead of the country where the attack occurred, so further analysis should be conducted. Utilizing a Poisson regression, openness to trade was found to have a positive relationship with the number of terrorist attacks [22].

Another potential proxy for economic fragility is economic growth. Research has shown that growth in real GDP is negatively correlated with terrorist attacks [22]. Coupling these results with the finding that in Africa, transnational terrorism has a negative relationship with economic growth [5], shows that terrorism and economic

17

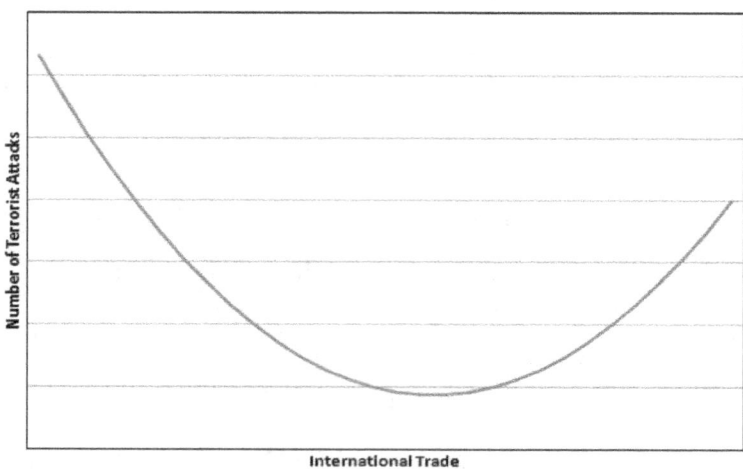

Figure 2. Notionalized relationship between the number of terrorist attacks and amount of international trade

growth create a negative feedback loop resulting in greater amount of terrorism and lower levels of economic growth.

The final factor is social fragmentation. Social fragmentation is the splintering of a country's populace into distinct portions. Usually these portions are upset with the government, when they under represented and consequently put down by the government. When a terrorist group operates against the government, the people who share their views (i.e. religious, cultural) are much more likely to support the terrorists. This fragmentation is a common source of civil conflict and the presence of civil conflict increases the quantity of terrorist attacks as well based upon a Poisson panel estimation [24].

A case study of the Taliban supports the proposed realtionship between terrorism and fragmentation [28]. In early 2006, the Taliban used the following five slogans to gain members: 1. "Our party, the Taliban" 2. "Our people and nation, the Pashtun" 3. "Our economy, the poppy" 4. "Our constitution, the Shari'a" 5. "Our form of government, the emirate". These slogans are used as "rallying calls" to gain supporters. Clearly, the Taliban uses its propaganda to bring in people that want their own political party, their own ethnicity as a nation, that have been prevented from making a living by growing poppies, from people agreeing with their religion, and wanting a new government.

While this case study shows how terrorists have capitalized on fragmentation. Poisson panel estimation analysis in regards to religion show that a larger percentage of Christians or a larger percentage of Muslims in the population correspond to an increased number of terrorist attacks [24]. However, Street also recorded that a larger Jewish population resulted in less attacks, which likely occurred since the analysis only looked at attacks for non-state actors. This analysis only focused on fragmentation in terms of religion, but it is clear that further analysis on social fragmentation and its potential relationship to terrorism is needed.

Review of Additional Variables.

The factors highlighted in Carter's analysis need further quantitative investigation, but the literature also contains other variables and relationships of note that will be reviewed in this section.

The literature debates whether some variables have a relationship with terrorist attacks. One of these highly contentious variables is the level of democracy in a country. The U.S. government has stated numerous times that an increase in democracy, leads to a decrease in terrorism [4, 14]. However, a negative binomial regression returned results that the level of democracy has no effect on the number of terrorist attacks [27]. Li, using pooled time series, and Street, using Poisson panel analyses, reported an increasing relationship with the number of terrorist attacks [21, 24].

Another potential reason for the opposing results could be that terrorism databases usually access public media to record terrorist attacks, so a democratic country would report these attacks more often than other types of governments. In order to determine the underlying causes of democracy, Li breaks up democracy into numerous representative factors [29]. Using a negative binomial regression, Li's results showed a positive relationship between freedom of the press, amount of government constraints, number of regime changes and the number of terrorist attacks. It is important to note that freedom of the press was added to the model in order to account for underreporting bias.

The vast majority of datasets recording terrorist attacks are based upon media sources. Since countries with freedom of the press report more attacks than their counterparts, adding freedom of the press to models to account for this underreporting bias is a common tactic [30]. There was a negative relationship between voter turnout, citizen satisfaction, electoral participation, and the number of terrorist attacks. By breaking democracy into constituent components, Li provided insight to what is truly going on with the relationship between democracy and terrorist attacks. This approach could be used on some of the other debated variables in the literature to display the underlying reasoning behind the results.

Since the DHS uses population density as an indicator for potential terrorists attacks, the organization apparently expects more attacks to occur in cities than anywhere else. It would be wise to further analyze cities if anything other than size of the city is a factor related to terrorist attacks. Research shows that a city with an aging infrastructure, such as roads and housing are more likely to have terrorist attacks than their modern counterparts. Additionally, cities are more vulnerable based upon the topographical location and layout of the city [31]. These indicators show the kinds of targets that terrorists seek out whether consciously or unconsciously. Lastly, location ended up being one of the major factors of determination between a city that is vulnerable to an attack and a city that is relatively safe from an attack [31]. This shows that very specific factors play a large role in terrorist attacks at the local level and it would be in the best interest of the DHS to identify more of these factors. These indicators are very insightful, but are unhelpful in terms of analysis at the country level.

The amount of education is another commonly analyzed factor. Street shows a positive correlation between the number of terrorist attacks and the average years of education achieved in a country, but goes on to comment that this is likely due to the beliefs and principles of the school systems in the country [24]. Using a Poisson regression instead of a panel regression, Street showed that education level has a negative relationship with terrorism, except in Europe and Islamic countries were the relationship is insignificant and positive, respectively [22]. This last analysis shows the importance of analyzing the world by region.

Regional differences are important to consider when analyzing terrorism due to various factors that differ from region to region (i.e. tactics, government, climate, etc.). Analyzing only southeastern Turkey highlighted that an economy based upon agriculture and government services have a relationship with the number of terrorist attacks in the region [32]. Examining different geographic regions can also return opposing results. For instance, level of investment and number of patents are negatively correlated with terrorism in the entire world, but have a positive reelationship in Islamic countries. Clearly, location is a very important factor which should be analyzed to better understand terrorist attacks.

There is also a debate whether U.S. foreign policy has any relationship with terrorism. The U.S. government states that no relationship exists [14], however another study utilizing principle components analysis and factor analysis showed that an unpopular U.S. foreign policy causes the U.S. to be a common driver of transnational terrorism [33]. It is interesting to note that a positive relationship was found between contributions to the U.N. budget of the victim country and the number of terrorist attacks using a zero-inflated negative binomial regression [25]. There is likely a relationship between U.S. or coalition membership foreign policy and terrorist attacks. As done previously with democracy, it may be beneficial to break up U.S. foreign policy into its constituent properties to determine any hidden relationships.

After exploring these different variable relationships, our research will set out on exploratory analysis to find additional variables and define their relationship to terrorism.

Survey Paper Review.

An extensive research effort has been conducted to explore these relationships. However, the size of this research has grossly out scaled consolidation efforts to compile all of this research into a simple form. The most recent consolidation efforts include a survey paper titled "What causes terrorism?", by Krieger and Meierrieks [34], and another working paper titled "Lock, stock and barrel: A comprehensive assessment of the determinants of terror" [1]. While these papers are very detailed and thorough in their consolidation efforts, there is room for improvement. First, the newest paper analyzed is from the year 2011 and this is only one paper. This means that a lot of recent research on terrorism has not been considered and additional consolidation should occur to update the consolidation. Second, neither paper focuses upon the quantitative methods used to capture these relationships. Therefore, this paper will first summarize the findings in these two survey papers. Then, an assessment of recent literature will be conducted to update these consolidation efforts. Lastly, a literature assessment of methodologies used to find the relationships between variables and terrorist attacks will be assessed and compiled.

"What causes terrorism?".

Krieger and Meierrieks are two respected names in terrorism research and have multiple publications in the area. This survey paper was published in 2011, but only contains sources from 2010 and before. However, this paper references 96 other papers and consolidates their findings into four areas. These four areas include sources of transnational terrorism, targets of transnational terrorism, domestic terrorism, and research that does not specify the type of terrorism [34]. In may variable relationships research comes to different conclusions. This paper specifies economic deprivation, modernization strain, political and institutional order, political transformation and instability, identity and culture clash, global economic and public order, and contagion. The authors explain the different findings in the research with the following five reasons:

1. Different dependent variables

2. Different data sources (ITERATE, MIPT, RAND)

3. Different time periods

4. Different exploratory variables

5. Different methodologies

Despite all of these reasons for debate among variable relationships, the survey paper found a few synonymous findings. Most of these findings occur because only one paper analyzed the specific variable. In regards to being sources of terrorism, some of these relationship include a positive relationship in regards to unequal alliances in power and a negative relationship in regards to World Trade Organization membership. Two researchers agreed that receiving foreign aid decreases being a source of terrorism.

23

In regards to being a target of terrorism, one article confirms a positive relationship with being in recession, youth burden, population density, illiteracy, new democracies, unfair balance of trade, and linguistic diversity. Two or more findings included a negative relationship for income inequality and regime stability and a positive relationship with state failure.

In unspecified terrorism, more than three articles agreed that contagion, or lagged autoregressive term, promotes terrorist attacks both temporally and spatially. Additionally, it is important to note that fourteen articles agreed that population has a positive effect on terrorism, but one paper came to the opposite conclusion.

"Lock, stock and barrel: A comprehensive assessment of the determinants of terror".

Gassebner and Luechinger's paper entitled "Lock, Stock, and Barrel: A comprehensive assessment of the determinants of terror" is a much more comprehensive survey of modern literature [1]. However, this is a working paper from 2011 and only references one paper from that year. The other 107 referenced articles were written before 2011. This paper breaks up terrorism into three categories of analysis: analysis based upon where the attacks occurred, analysis based upon the targets, or victims, of the attack, and analysis on the perpetrators of the attack. This review of the literature produced 65 correlates that were re-assessed for robustness. These variables were re-assessed using Extreme Bound Analysis, which compares "commonly accepted" variables to variables of interest. The "commonly accepted" variables include GDP per capita, population size and level of democracy, since these are the most commonly analyzed variables in the literature. The authors recorded the percentage of regressions where the variables of interest were significantly different zero to assess robustness. Robustness is defined as scoring above a 90% and this robustness score is checked for the three common data sources (MIPT, ITERATE, and GTD) and variants of these datasets related to aspects of terrorism.

Due to the comprehensive assessment, this paper has many results of interest. First, the degree of democracy and GDP per capita are not robustly associated with terrorism. This result is very interesting since so much research disputes these specific variables. Second, the authors found 18 variables that are robust based upon location of the attack, 15 associated with the targets of the attack, and 6 related to the perpetrators of the attack. Of the 18 variables based upon location only physical integrity rights and religious tension are robust for all three data sources with a negative and positive relationship, respectively. Population size, economic freedom and infant mortality rate came to the same conclusion for two of the data sets. These results as well as the other 13 robust variables can be found in Table 1.

For the analysis focused on the victims and perpetrators of terrorism, economic freedom (negative relationship), physical integrity rights (negative relationship), and having an internal war supported by external countries (positive relationship) all come to the same conclusion for all three data sets. The results of this analysis can be seen in Table 2.

While these papers do provide a broad overview of terrorism literature, they do not capture more recent research, since they were both written in 2011. Consequently, a broad overview on some articles that were not included in these survey papers will be conducted.

Methodologies to find relationships between characteristics and terrorist attacks.

Within the terrorism analysis literature, many different methodologies are used from systems thinking to game theory and from comparisons of means to multivariate

Table 1. Lock, Stock, and Barrel: results of location focused EBA analysis [1]

Variable	Location, ITERATE			Location, GTD			Location, MIPT		
	Coef.	CDF	% sig.	Coef.	CDF	% sig.	Coef.	CDF	% sig.
Baseline variables									
GDP per capita, log	0.103	0.681	39.6	0.210	0.894	73.4	0.063	0.628	27.6
Population, log	0.142	0.837	62.3	0.221	**0.984**	93.7	0.177	**0.902**	68.8
Democracy	0.059	0.550	23.7	0.191	0.646	48.9	-0.065	0.537	14.7
Partial Democracy	0.035	0.542	20.9	0.225	0.726	53.0	-0.017	0.523	10.2
Robust variables									
Physical integrity	-0.138	**0.979**	92.1	-0.165	**0.970**	90.8	-0.099	**0.914**	73.5
Religious tension	0.103	**0.934**	80.6	0.121	**0.986**	96.3	0.069	**0.918**	74.6
Economic freedom	-0.307	**0.948**	80.0	-0.269	**0.949**	83.0	-0.327	0.899	71.7
Infant mortality	-0.017	**0.910**	67.2	-0.010	**0.903**	64.1	-0.008	0.699	22.4
Ethnic tensions	-0.007	0.544	18.4	0.040	**0.911**	63.1	0.011	0.627	15.2
Gvt. fractionalization	0.450	0.867	64.9	0.420	**0.919**	73.5	0.411	0.852	60.8
Guerrilla war	0.208	0.877	65.7	0.370	**0.990**	96.0	0.182	0.893	62.3
Internal war	0.086	0.839	46.5	0.264	**0.987**	95.6	0.112	0.856	62.4
Internat. internal war	0.028	0.624	6.5	0.147	**0.933**	69.6	0.059	0.735	14.0
Law and order	0.002	0.538	11.6	-0.072	**0.960**	82.3	-0.059	0.882	62.8
Military expenditures	0.027	0.701	29.1	0.079	**0.935**	79.8	0.015	0.625	17.2
Military personnel	0.041	0.791	32.2	0.077	**0.923**	73.1	0.025	0.691	21.5
OECD	-0.108	0.600	14.2	0.407	**0.914**	68.4	0.137	0.661	11.0
Portfolio investment	1.029	0.743	7.4	0.037	0.539	1.8	2.877	**0.963**	80.4
Proximity to U.S.	1.266	0.813	42.8	1.481	**0.905**	72.0	0.969	0.795	34.6
Strikes	0.068	0.810	37.6	0.126	**0.906**	75.5	0.088	0.897	53.1
Urbanization	0.015	0.856	62.7	0.005	0.716	42.3	0.023	**0.913**	77.5

Note: The table reports the median parameter estimates (Coef.), the cumulative distribution function (CDF), i.e. the proportion of the cumulative distribution function lying on each side of zero, and the percent the estimate was statistically significant at the 5% level (% sig.). The criterion to consider a variable robustly related to terrorism is a CDF above .9 which is printed in **bold** face.

Table 2. Lock, Stock, and Barrel: results of victim and perpetrator focused EBA analysis [1]

Variable	Victim, ITERATE			Victim, GTD			Perpetrator, ITERATE		
	Coef.	CDF	% sig.	Coef.	CDF	% sig.	Coef.	CDF	% sig.
Baseline variables									
GDP per capita, log	0.304	0.852	58.5	0.371	**0.957**	87.9	-0.020	0.528	21.0
Population, log	0.307	**0.965**	90.0	0.247	**0.990**	96.6	0.111	0.774	38.8
Democracy	-0.111	0.599	10.6	-0.018	0.512	40.1	-0.327	0.755	37.9
Partial Democracy	-0.196	0.741	21.7	0.041	0.556	29.1	-0.110	0.629	23.3
Robust variables									
Economic freedom	-0.313	**0.938**	83.3	-0.202	**0.914**	73.0	-0.374	**0.954**	82.1
Internat. internal war	0.188	**0.963**	85.1	0.134	**0.927**	70.3	0.169	**0.906**	60.5
Physical integrity	-0.101	**0.969**	85.2	-0.137	**0.935**	82.4	-0.198	**0.985**	93.5
Guerrilla war	0.098	0.766	28.2	0.366	**0.993**	97.2	0.325	**0.935**	77.5
Internal war	0.170	**0.930**	73.7	0.270	**0.987**	95.1	0.126	0.874	59.7
Telephone	0.006	0.720	16.9	0.019	**0.934**	80.7	-0.026	**0.934**	72.8
Centrist government	0.117	0.783	30.2	-0.069	0.721	20.8	0.294	**0.936**	63.0
Ethnic tensions	-0.007	0.582	7.5	0.039	**0.909**	65.2	-0.006	0.527	12.5
Military expenditures	0.026	0.643	10.5	0.074	**0.917**	78.5	0.028	0.648	18.5
OECD	-0.345	0.789	33.0	0.717	**0.976**	90.4	-0.329	0.729	28.1
Proximity to U.S.	0.854	0.758	28.6	2.233	**0.968**	88.8	1.377	0.801	33.9
Primary goods exports	-0.006	0.786	34.4	-0.007	**0.930**	72.7	0.001	0.536	10.6
Religious tensions	0.063	0.841	62.5	0.124	**0.987**	96.7	0.071	0.858	53.3
Youth bulge	-4.604	0.830	58.5	-4.504	**0.930**	78.9	1.398	0.619	26.1

Note: The table reports the median parameter estimates (Coef.), the cumulative distribution function (CDF), i.e. the proportion of the cumulative distribution function lying on each side of zero, and the percent the estimate was statistically significant at the 5% level (% sig.). The criterion to consider a variable robustly related to terrorism is a CDF above .9 which is printed in **bold face**.

techniques. Since different methodologies can lead to different conclusions, the topic of methodologies is very important. The research questions laid out in Section 1.3 can be answered using a variety of strategies. By analyzing the methodologies of others, it is possible to determine what works well, what may not work, and other strategies to overcome common problems.

One of these techniques is to analyze the interaction between the United States and terrorists through game theory, which helps to capture the action and reaction of the players [18]. While conducting this analysis certainly is a step in the right direction, this does not fix the previously mentioned problems of being unable to determine every scenario and the likelihood of that scenario. Furthermore, classical game theory is difficult to apply to this problem because the desired outcomes of terrorists and the U.S. government greatly differ from each other. Additionally, the utilities and objectives are very different for different types of terrorist groups. For instance, a nuclear attack on American soil has a greater benefit for al-Qa'ida than a disgruntled American [18]. The changes in tactics by an intelligent adversary, the changing political and economic environments as well as new and changing sources of intelligence make it difficult to apply game theory to terrorist attacks. However, game theory analysis does attempt to take the current knowledge about terrorism and apply it to U.S. strategy, so it is a step in the right direction.

Another method is to use a systems thinking based approach. Schoenenberger et. al. [35] used this approach to analyze terrorism as a system and compartmentalized it into recruitment, impact of attack, media, resources, and a negative view of industrialized nations [35]. This approach has advantages, especially in determining portions of the system to infiltrate. However, it lacks the quantitative rigor necessary to determine which relationships will provide insight into the terrorist choices in targets.

Since this research is based upon the relationships between certain country characteristics and the total number of terrorist attacks, multivariate techniques can aid in discovering underlying patterns in historical terrorist attacks. However, even within multivariate techniques, many potential options exist and are applicable to this problem. Some of the methodologies currently analyzed in the literature include negative binomial or Poisson regression techniques, both with and without the zero-inflated specification, benchmark analysis using logit or probit models, classification trees, and principle components analysis.

Due to the nature of the data, many individuals have not used a simple linear regression technique. However, many other regression techniques have been used. One potential methodology is to use a negative binomial regression [27, 29]. Additionally, some researchers' data on terrorist attacks contained a large number of zeros, causing them to conduct a zero-inflated negative binomial regression [25, 36]. While the negative binomial regression is the most common technique, others various regression techniques have been used including a pooled time series regression [21], a cross-sectional time series regression [30], a mixed effects Poisson regression model [22, 37], or a Poisson panel estimation [24].

A benchmark analysis is another potential regression technique. In order to assess urban vulnerability to terrorist attacks, a model was created that was able to determine cities with a vulnerability above 50%, which would be a very useful tool for the DHS [31]. For this specific model, having a vulnerability above 50% means that at least one terrorist attack is likely to occur in the city. Other researchers have used this same benchmark, but have used logit and probit models to determine whether an attack is likely to occur in a specified region [32, 37].

Classification trees, similar to the benchmark analysis, seek cutoff points among variables. Depending on the analysis, being on one end of this cutoff describes the

Table 3. Summary of Literature Review by Methodology

	Linear Regression	Negative Binomial	Tobit	Markhov Process	Mean Comparisons	Logit	Poisson	Systems Thinking
Number of Articles	7	36	8	1	3	3	2	1
Percentage of Articles	11.5%	59.0%	13.1%	1.6%	4.9%	4.9%	3.3%	1.6%

expected relationship with terrorist attacks. A classification tree was conducted based upon terrorist attacks and their relationship to the type, strength, and stability of a government [38]

Principal Component Analysis (PCA) is helpful in determining important relationships between variables and the number of terrorist attacks. This technique was used to identify the important socio-economic characteristics that have a relationship with terrorist attacks in Southeast Turkey [32]. Additionally, this technique was coupled with factor analysis to determine which countries are drivers of transnational terrorism; terrorist activity in one or more countries serve as an indicator of terrorist attacks at the global scale [33].

Table 3 summarizes the findings from the Gassebner and Luechinger survey paper and additional studies from this literature review by methodology [1].

Clearly, the negative binomial is the standard for most analyses with well over 50% of the surveyed articles, but simply being used more does not mean it is the most accurate model. The second most common model is the Tobit model, which analyzes censored data; it is important to note that all eight articles include the author S.B. Bloomberg [1]. Seven individuals used an ordinary least squares analysis approach. It is interesting to note that many researchers conclude that the data is not normally distributed and is not continuous since it is count data. If this is true, both the Tobit and OLS models are inadequate techniques, since they both demand that errors are normally distributed with constant variance and a mean of zero. Three articles also conducted a logistic model. This is a sensible technique, but demands that a specified cutoff be used in the analysis. This cutoff could be a specified number of attacks or whether or not attacks occur. Since the data suffers from underreporting bias [30], it can be difficult to determine which numbers are truly zero or truly small, and therefore, choosing a cutoff can be a very difficult process. Additionally, this methodology does not predict the quantity of terrorist attacks. The last commonly used methodology is mean comparison. This technique is very basic and is fundementally used in almost all of the other common techniques.

Clearly, using the negative binomial regression is the most common technique used in the literature analysis of terrorist attacks with socio-economic variables. The fact that so many different researchers used the same methodology helps to validate the methodology, but this does not mean it is the most appropiate methodology. It is also important to note that the count for negative binomial does not specify between the standard negative binomial distribution and the zero-inflated adaptation. These last two points show the importance of conducting data specific analysis to determine the most appropiate technique.

2.5   Model Selection Metrics

The performance of models, is gauged using certain metrics and statistical tests. Through these metrics and statistical tests, it is possible to compare and contrast different models to determine the best model.

Metrics.

Akaike Information Criterion.

The first metric commonly used for model selection is Akaike Information Criterion (AIC). This metric balances how well a model fits the data with model complexity, measured by the number of independent variables. The metric is based upon Equation 1,

$$AIC = -2\ln(L) + 2k \qquad (1)$$

where k is the number of parameters in the model and L is the maximized value for the likelihood function [39]. A likelihood function is based upon information theory and uses known outcome data to evaluate the relationship with independent data [40]. The log of the maximum of the likelihood function, which is commonly referred to as the log-likelihood, simply scales the maximum value to allow for simpler derivation. As seen above, the log-likelihood is multipled by negative two, while the number of parameters is multiplied by positive two. Since a better model has a large likelihood with fewer parameters, the better model has the lower value for AIC. This metric only has an interpretation relative to another model's metric.

Bayesian Information Criterion.

The second metric for model comparison is Bayesian Information Criteria (BIC). Similar to AIC, BIC balances model fit and complexity, but instead is based upon Equation 2,

$$BIC = -2\ln(L) + \ln(n)k \qquad (2)$$

where k is the number of parameters in the model and L is the maximized value for the likelihood function just like AIC. The only difference between the two is k, the number of parameters, is multiplied by the natural log of n, which is the data sample size. Consequently, BIC gives more weight to model complexity relative to AIC as long as there are more than seven data points. Just like AIC, the metric for BIC must be compared relative to another model's BIC calculation and the better model has a smaller BIC.

Root Mean Square Error.

Another commonly used metric for model comparison is the root mean square error. In regression, errors are synomous with a term referred to as a residual. Both of these terms simply mean the difference between the prediction by the model and the actual data. In order to assess the performance of a model, these errors are commonly squared, to account for negatives and provide heavier weight to missed data, and then summed into one metric. This one number is referred to as the sum of square error (SSE). This number provides worse results for problems with more data points, since their will be more error terms. Consequently, it is common to divide SSE by the number of data points to get mean square error (MSE). Since the errors were squared, the units for MSE are also squared. Consequently, it is common to take the square root of the MSE to put units into easily interpretable terms. This metric is called the RMSE and is the same calculation as the sample standard deviation. It can be seen in Equation 3.

$$\text{RMSE} = \sqrt{\frac{\sum_{t=1}^{n}(\hat{y}_t - y)^2}{n}} \tag{3}$$

There are a few different applications of RMSE which relay different information about the model. First, there is an RMSE based upon model fit. The RMSE based upon model fit comes from the data used to build the model. This RMSE is constructed to have the smallest SSE, because the model is built to have the smallest error terms. When RMSE is calculated on validation data that was not used to create the model, this metric really assesses the robustness and appropriateness of the model in application to data outside of the sample used to construct the model. When the RMSE is used in a cross-validation, the RMSE really addresses the predictive power of the model, since the validation data is coming from a test set of data.

Log-likelihood Test.

While it is common to compare different metrics across model, there are also instances when hypothesis testing can be used to determine the most appropriate model. One of these hypothesis tests is the log-likelihood test. This test assesses two models where one model is nested inside of the other. These models are compared to see if the additional parameters are necessary to explain a difference in variation. The hypothesis test has the following format:

Null Hypothesis: The simpler model is appropriate

Alternative Hypothesis: The general model is appropriate

The test statistic is distributed χ^2, where the degrees of freedom is equivalent to the difference in the number of parameters between the two models. This statistic is easily turned into a p-value to determine which model is more appropriate.

Cross-Validation.

Finding relationships between specific variables and terrorist attacks is useful to better understanding terrorist attacks, but in order for this information to be useful and not by chance correlated, these relationships must have predictive power. Finding relationships with predictive power, provides a gateway to shaping policies that affect the variable, and consequently, affect terrorism.

In order to evaluate predictive power of any model, we must first fit the model, then make a prediction and finally estimate the prediction error. "The most widely used method for estimating prediction error is cross-validation" [41]. Validation, involves a subset of the data used to evaluate the predictive capability of the model. However, when data are scarce, another validation techniques is k-fold cross-validation.

K-fold cross-validation splits the data into k independent portions. A model is constructed based upon all of the portions except one, and that last portion of the data is used for validation. This process continues until all portions of the data have been used for validation. The value used for k should be chosen carefully, as this value balances the amount of variance and bias in the model. If k is equivalent to the number of data points, this technique is called a leave-one-out cross-validation and minimizes bias, while having the most variance between the k validations [41].

One large challenge with k-fold cross-validation is that the data must be split into k independent portions. This is impossible to do when the data are dependent upon each other as it usually is in most time-based prediction scenerios. In order to cope with this issue, it is common to use another technique called blocked cross-validation.

Blocked Cross-Validation.

Blocked cross-validation divides the data into identically distributed, but not independent blocks [42]. In time-based models, these blocks are usually one or more time steps. The first block is used to build a model, which is validated with the second block. Then both of these blocks are used to build a model that validates the third block. This process continues until the final block of data is validated. This technique produces predictive errors at every time step, in order to analyze the predicitve power of the model.

III. Confirmatory Analysis

3.1 Overview

This chapter investigates the first research question from Section 1.3:

- Can the qualitative relationships considered indicators of terrorism be quantitatively supported with a generalized linear model?

3.2 Data Collection

The charachteristics of terrorism outlined in "Pre-incident Indicators of Terrorist Attacks: Weak Economies and Fragile Political Infrastructure Bring Rise to Terrorist Organizations and Global Networks", by Carter, is quantitatively assessed in this chapter. This article identified five indicators that claim to serve as pre-incident indicators of terrorism and are summarized in Section 2.4. It is important to note that Carter's analysis draws on social science literature. This chapter statistically tests the indicators indentified by Carter, to see if they can be quantitatively supported. To quantitatively support the findings in Carter's article, we use data that accurately depicts modern day terrorist attacks and data that accurately represents Carter's five factors.

Terrorism Data.

The data representing terrorist attacks came from the Global Terrorism Database (GTD), maintained by the National Consortium for the Study of Terrorism and Responses to Terrorism (START). This database contains a list of terrorist attacks dating back to 1970. To be considered a terrorist attack, an event must meet the inclusion criteria for the GTD. This inclusion criteria is based on the consortium's definition of terrorism, which can be found in Section 2.1.

This data was collected using an extensive review of publicly available, unclassified, open source materials. These materials include media articles, electronic news articles, existing data sets, books, journals, and legal documents [11]. Only events that meet the aforementioned inclusion criteria are recorded as terrorist attacks in the GTD.

For this research, the event data was the aggregated number of terrorist attacks occurring in a year (1 Jan to 31 Dec) for each African country.

Factor Data.

Data is needed to evaluate Carter's five factors. Since Carter's factors reference concepts and ideas instead of quantitative measurements, each factor is represented by a proxy variable. The source and selection processes for these proxy variables are described below.

Poverty.

Poverty is commonly analyzed in terrorism research using GDP per capita as a proxy variable. Despite the common use of GDP per capita, it is a poor proxy for poverty, especially when better alternatives are available. GDP per capita does not describe as much about poverty as it does the ratio of economic output to the population. Additionally, GDP per capita does not state anything about the actual spread of the country's wealth, but assumes that it is equal. Past research found the Gini Index, which measures income inequality, statistically significant, the assumption of equal distribution of wealth is unlikely to be valid. The Gini Index does not measure poverty, but income inequality, and therefore, is a poor proxy for Carter's definition.

The proxy variable for poverty used is the percentage of people living below a $2 a day poverty line. This indicator choice is believed to better represent true poverty and provides an equivalent cutoff for all countries. An alternative could be to use the national poverty line, but it is inconsistent from country to country. This data came from the World Bank.

Lack of Border Control.

There are no intuitive databases describing border security between countries in Africa, especially as assessment that changed over time. Consideration was given to analyzing migration rates, tariff rates, and even illegal drug or arms trade data were considered as potential proxy variables. However, all of these data sets were unreliable, not readily accessible, or did not truly represent border control as a proxy variable.

The Fragile State Index ranks countries to determine which countries are weak or failing. In order to do this they "convert millions of pieces of information into a form that is relevant as well as easily digestible and informative [43]." These millions of pieces of information are quantified into over one hundred sub-indicators, which are aggregated to 12 main indicators, which are once again aggregated to form the overall country score. These 12 main indicators examine social, economic, political, and military examples including uneven economic development, external intervention, and public services to name a few [43].

The security apparatus indicator measures the "extent to which the social contract is weakened by competing groups, which is a proxy measure of security in a country [43]. While this indicator does not speak to border control, every border is shared by two or more countries. By looking at the surrounding countries, more insight into border control is provided. Therefore, the indicator for border security is the sum product of the bordering country's security apparatus score and the percentage of border shared with that country. For example, the United States score would be the security apparatus score for Canada multiplied by the percent of land border shared with Canada plus the security apparatus score for Mexico multiplied by the percent of land border shared with Mexico.

Political Corruption.

The proxy for political corruption comes from state legitimacy indicator of the Fragile State Index. State legitimacy measures the "corruption and lack of representativeness in the government" [43].

Economic Fragility.

A proxy for economic fragility is the economic vulnerability index built by the United Nations and Ferdi. This index measures the "structural vulnerability of countries to exogenous economic and environmental shocks" [44]. This proxy better approximates economic fragility as opposed to other proxies such as integration into global economy, international trade, or GDP. Consequently, it more adequately represents economic fragility.

Social Fragmentation.

The proxy for social fragmentation comes from group grievance indicator of the Fragile State Index. Group grievance measures the "tension and violence exists between groups" [43]. The benefit of using this index as opposed to other indicators is that this measure includes ethnic, religious, and power fragmentation, instead of focusing on one type of fragmentation.

3.3 Data Treatment

All collected data were processed prior to analysis.

Missing Data.

Data was specifically chosen for its availability. However, some of the five factor data contained missing values. These missing values were a result of the Fragile State Index not evaluating the country or from World Bank and the United Nations not collecting or reporting data every year.

In order to fill these missing values, the k nearest neighbors data imputation technique was used. This technique looks across the multivariate space at the statistically closest data points to the missing data point based upon Mahalanobis distance. The missing data point is estimated based upon a weighted average of a specified number of points. This analysis used the ten closest points for data imputation, k=10, which is commonly used and the default for the "impute" package in R. Only two independent variables, EVI and poverty, were missing values. EVI had 49 missing data points, which is about a 15% of the data. However, poverty was missing approximately 80% of the data points. Since both variables were related to economic condition of the country, GDP per capita was temporarily appended to the dataset in order to have more accurate imputations based upon economic data and then removed before analysis. This technique successfully filled the data set with reasonable values allowing the analysis to continue unabated.

Data Standardization.

Lastly, the data was standardized to simplify comparisons. Additionally, standardizing and mean-correcting help address potential multicollinearity issues within the data. Consequently, the data was both mean differenced and corrected for variance.

3.4 Scope and Assumptions

This section outlines both the assumptions and scope of the problem.

Analysis of Africa.

Much research has been conducted on terrorism at the global level and at the small regional level such as south-eastern Turkey and specific states within the U.S. Conducting research at the global level does not find relationships that are specific to a region. Some research has attempted to use dummy variables to find these regional trends; however, using a dummy variable does not account for the effect of each growth determinant [5]. Conducting analysis at the regional level provides specific relationships, but is not robust to general trends or applicable to a large area. For the reasons outlined in Section 1.2, the continent of Africa was the clear choice for this analysis.

Country Removal.

Currently, Africa contains 53 countries including the surrounding islands. The country of South Sudan came into existence in 2011 and was removed from the dataset due to a lack of data for both the dependent and independent variables. For this study Sudan and South Sudan are aggregated for both independent and dependent data. South Sudan is used seperately in the analysis when calculating spatial variables, such as border security, for its bordering countries. Future analysis should include South Sudan as an independent country due to its lack of stability based upon being the most fragile state in 2014 [43]. Additionally, some states are very small based upon population. Further examination of these countries shows that the majority of them do not have an autonomous government or are in heavily disputed territory. In order to reduce the effect of the analysis being dependent upon countries outside of Africa or issues related to small population, all countries with current populations less than a million are removed except for Djibouti. Since Djibouti is strategically significant to the United States, has an autonomous government, and is the closest country to the million population cutoff, it is retained in the model. This results in 49 African countries in the analysis.

Analysis Time Period.

Lastly, it is important to define the time period that the analysis will span. The GTD contains event data back to February 1968 to 2013, except for the year 1993. However, terrorism has drastically changed over this time period. David Kilcullen stated that modern terrorists differ significantly in "policy, strategy, operational art, and tactical technique," as well as wealth and urbanization compared to past terrorist organizations [2]. To get an accurate depiction of modern terrorism, it is important to analyze terrorism in recent times. Since this analysis is focused upon Africa, it is vital to analyze factors which shape terrorism in Africa. Two large events occurred in 2007 that caused a shift in Africa and in terrorism across the continent. In February 2007, the AFRICOM combat command was created, showing increased U.S. interest in Africa [6]. Also in 2007, the U.S. troop surge in Iraq supporting operation eduring freedom and operation Iraqi freedom was implemented. This increase of troops was viewed by many as successful in dealing with terrorism based upon a decrease in U.S. troop fatalities and terrorist attacks in Iraq. This means that terrorists were either placed on the defensive or escaped to other countries. Either way, this event effected terrorism on both a global and regional scale. Due to these events and the desire to analyze recent terrorism, the analysis time period will go from 1 Jan 2007 until 31 Dec 2013.

3.5 Methodology

Model Types.

While methodology among terrorism studies ranges from systems thinking [35] to Principal Component Analysis [5, 32], many researchers choose to conduct regression techniques. Within regression techniques, researchers commonly use a Poisson, a negative binomial, or a zero-inflated negative binomial regression, with the negative binomial regressions being the most popular [1]. A negative binomial regression is very similar to linear regression. However, instead of assuming that the residuals are normally distributed, the assumption is that the residuals are negatively binomially distributed. This means that the probability mass function is defined by Equation 4 [45],

$$\Pr(X = k) = \left(\frac{r}{r+\mu}\right)^{r} \frac{\Gamma(r+k)}{k!\,\Gamma(r)} \left(\frac{\mu}{r+\mu}\right)^{k} \quad \text{for } k = 0, 1, 2, \ldots \quad (4)$$

where μ is the mean, $\mu + \frac{\mu^2}{r}$ is the variance, and r is the dispersion parameter. Unlike a Poisson regression model, the mean is not equivalent to the variance for the negative binomial, which is mainly driven by the dispersion parameter. For this data, $\mu=16$ and $\sigma^2=3{,}250$ The dispersion parameter is calculated with the Iteratively Reweighted Least Squares (IRLS) algorithm. This algorithm finds the maximum likelihood estimates of a glm by iteratively solving a weighted least squares problem to find the dispersion parameter. The independent data is assumed to be independent from each other, which was confirmed by VIF scores less than 5, before mean-correcting the data. The incident, or dependent, data is assumed to be approximately stationary; meaning the variance between years is relatively low. Additionally, the dependent data in a negative binomial regression is log-linked to the independent data, which is equivalent to conducting a log transformation upon the model.

There are also zero-inflated versions of the Poisson and negative binomial regressions. These regressions are the same as the basic regressions, but add a logistic regression which splits the data into zero and non-zero values. This remedies regression errors due to excessive zeros. A histogram of the distribution of terrorist attacks can be seen in Figure 3. Clearly, the data contains numerous zeros, however, it is unclear if the amount of zeros demands the zero-inflated negative binomial or if the standard negative binomial distribution captures this quantity of zeros.

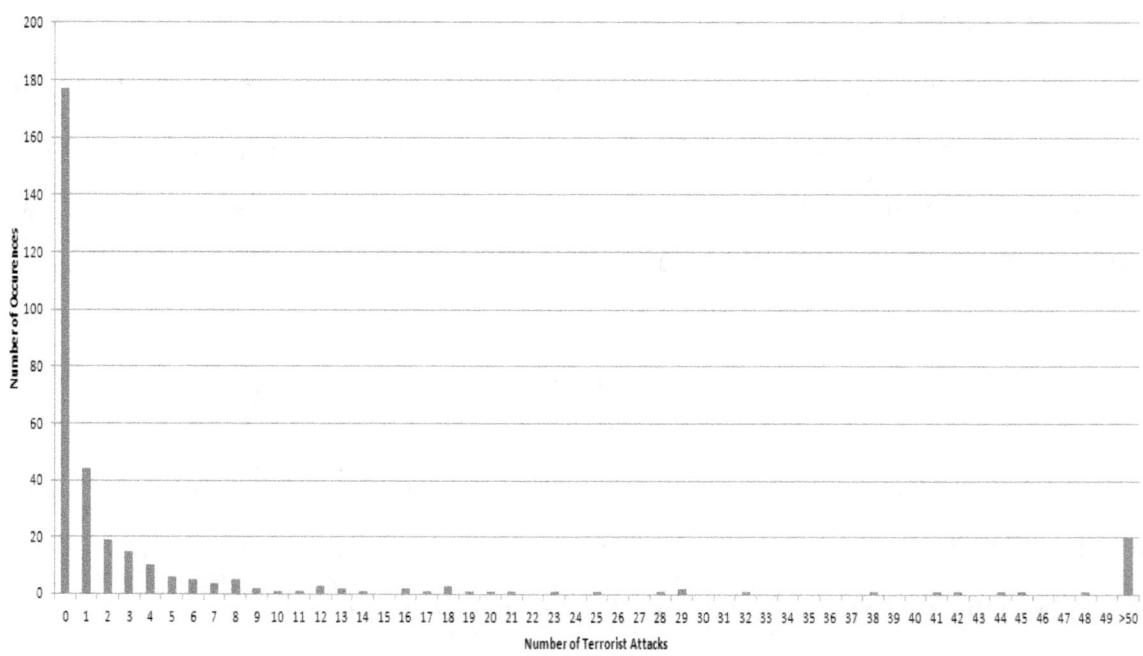

Figure 3. Occurence histogram of annual terrorist attacks

Model Evaluation.

Table 4 shows the results of the negative binomial regression using a full model, the zero-inflated negative binomial regression, a Poisson regression and the zero-inflated Poisson regression. The metrics in this table are described in Section 2.5.

Based upon AIC, the negative binomial regressions drastically outperform the Poisson models. BIC cannot be calculated for zero-inflated models, but these results

Table 4. Model comparisons among methodologies

	AIC	BIC	RMSE
NB	1606.27	1633.13	3.31
ZINB	1592.38	N/A	51.42
Poisson	14832.64	14855.67	3.22
ZIP	11625.16	N/A	50.78

once again show the negative binomial outperforming the Poisson regression. Lastly, in regards to the RMSE, the zero-inflated models perform poorly relative to the models without the zero-inflated portion. From an initial overall perspective, the negative binomial model seems to outperform the two Poisson models in terms of AIC, while it outperforms the two zero-inflated models from the RMSE perspective.

There are many reasons why some researchers have chosen to include the zero-inflated portion of the regression, while others have foregone it. Some of these reasons include knowledge of the zero-inflated portion and differences in the actual data set used. As the distribution previously showed, the data contains many zeros, but a comparison of both regression techniques must be conducted to determine if the data is truly zero-inflated.

In comparing the negative binomial (NB) regression to its zero-inflated counter-part, the zero-inflated negative binomial (ZINB) has a slightly lower AIC indicating a slightly better fitting model. However, analyzing the RMSE clearly shows the NB dominant to the ZINB; indicating NB is the better prediction model. Consequently, the data are best regressed upon using the negative binomial regression. This is likely due to the more recent time frame of this analysis in contrast to other research in the field. Since 1996, the average number of terrorist attacks has increased more than six-fold at the global level [3]. Also, this analysis has a lower proportion of zeros than other research which commonly analyze terrorism as far back as 1968. Additionally, since the analysis only looks at countries in Africa in contrast to the entire world. African countries may be less likely to report zero terrorist attacks than other countries around the world due to the lack of media control and the amount of foreign intervention. This causes less zero values in the data. While including the zero-inflated portion may be appropriate with other data sets, inclusion with this prediction model and variables did not yield the best results. Therefore, a negative binomial regression is used to analyze the data.

Results.

The results of the negative binomial regression are seen in Table 5. It is important to note that the inverse of the dispersion parameter, r, is represented by θ in the table. It's signifigance shows that the data is over-dispersed and the Negative Binomial is more appropiate than the Poisson regression.

When using regression techniques, it can be very difficult to differentiate between correlation and causation. This research is focused upon factors which can act as indicators of terrorism. In order to better analyze this relationship, each of the independent variables is lagged one year. For instance, terrorist attacks in 2007 are regressed on factor data from 2006. Therefore, the time for analyzing terrorist attacks will be from 2007 to 2013, but the independent variables will range from 2006 to 2012. This table shows all model factors with the exception of poverty significant at $\alpha=.05$. This shows that economic vulnerability, border security, fragmentation, and corruption are significant indicators of terrorism vulnerability.

3.6 Model Robustness

This model is also compared to the same model removing one factor at a time. These results are in Table 6. The best two models are retaining all factors and retaining all factors except for poverty. These two models have relatively equivalent

Table 5. Negative Binomial Regression Results

	Dependent variable:
	yterr
EVI	−0.361**
	(0.143)
Border.Security	0.402**
	(0.164)
Fragmented	1.207***
	(0.158)
Corruption	0.401**
	(0.160)
Poverty.percent.below.2USD	−0.169
	(0.133)
Constant	1.661***
	(0.130)
Observations	343
Log Likelihood	−797.135
θ	0.197*** (0.019)
Akaike Inf. Crit.	1,606.270
Note:	*p<0.1; **p<0.05; ***p<0.01

Table 6. Model comparisons witholding variables

Model	AIC	BIC
All	1606.27	1633.13
EVI Removed	1608.95	1631.98
Border Security Removed	1609.60	1632.63
Fragmentation Removed	1643.43	1666.46
Corruption Removed	1610.66	1633.69
Poverty Removed	1605.09	1628.11

performance, but it interesting to note that a log-likelihood test, addressed in Section 2.5, recommended the model without poverty with a p-value of 0.366.

As seen in Table 5, poverty does not have a significant relationship with the number of terrorist attacks. In the literature, much debate exists over whether or not a relationship exists between poverty and terrorism. However, those who do find a relationship, usually conclude that the relationship is small, so it is not surprising that poverty was not found to be a significant indicator of terrorism.

Interestingly, economic fragility appears to have a negative relationship with the number of terrorist attacks which is significant at $\alpha = .05$. This disagrees with Carter's explanation, which could be attributed to the use of a proxy variable. We believe this relationship occurs due to more stable, less fragile, economies serve as targets on the African continent.

Additionally, the proxy variables based upon the Fragile State Index are all statistically significant. It is important to remember that the higher component score on the Fragile State Index indicates higher fragility. Therefore, lack of border control has a significantly positive relationship with the number of terrorist attacks at $\alpha = .05$. This makes intuitive sense, but is the first time this relationship has been quantitatively supported. As fragmentation increases, the number of terrorist attacks

Table 7. Blocked cross-validation root mean square error results

RMSE	Full Model	EVI Removed	Border Security Removed	Fragmentation Removed	Corruption Removed	Poverty Removed
2008	52.2	80.8	42.2	40.5	54.8	30.5
2009	23.6	24.6	23.1	31.2	23.5	23.4
2010	22.3	21.8	22.0	27.6	21.7	21.3
2011	30.3	29.1	30.3	36.4	30.1	30.5
2012	87.9	86.6	88.1	94.8	87.7	87.9
2013	83.4	83.0	83.9	87.0	83.1	83.5
Overall	52.6	57.1	51.4	55.1	52.8	50.1

significantly increase at $\alpha = .01$. This also makes sense and agrees with the current literature. A similar relationship exists between corruption and the number of terrorist attacks except this relationship is only significant at $\alpha = .05$. This relationship is also intuitive and is supported in the literature as well.

3.7 Blocked Cross-Validation

As mentioned in Section 2.5, blocked cross-validation provides a systematic method to measure prediction error when data are both dependent and scarce. Therefore, a blocked cross-validation was conducted using years as the blocks. First, this analysis was conducted using the full model. Then, one of the five variables was removed and the blocked cross-validation was reconducted in order to see the difference in models using a subset of the variables. The results are in Table 7.

As expected, removing the variables with highly significant relationships causes an increase in RMSE, while removing weak relationships does not have a drastic impact on RMSE. For instance, removing fragmentation causes an increase in RMSE, while removing poverty improves the predictive power of the model.

Overtime, the model clearly loses predictive power as the RMSEs for 2012 and 2013 are drastically higher than in earlier years. Since blocked cross-validation builds the full model in time increments, a truly predictive model would exhibit a decrease in RMSE or at least RMSE would remain relatively the same as more time increments are included. Since the cross-validation RMSEs drastically increase after 2011, this model lacks predictive power. Additionally, a RMSE is interpreted to provide a rough range of prediction. Even the smallest RMSE values are greater than 20 and the largest exceed 90 terrorist attacks per country per year. In regards to this problem, over or under predicting the annual number of terrorist attacks for a single country by 50 attacks can have drastic consequences and these problems only become worse as the RMSE increases.

There are a few potential reasons for this lack in predictive capability. First, it is important to recall that proxies for Carter's five factors were analyzed, since the idealogical concepts could not be quantitatively tested. Second, Carter's factors come from an analysis of countries on the Arabian peninsula and the horn of Africa, while this paper looks at Africa collectively. Third, while many of Carter's factors were useful in predicting terrorism, there are likely to be additional variables that can improve the predictive capability. Regardless, this model lacks predictive power, especially to an extent for countries to adequately prepare for the upcoming year. An accurate predictive model is important as decisions are made on where to focus military aid, diplomatic attention, and other resources to counter the terrorism threat in Africa. Therefore, the other research questions will be addressed with the hope of improving the predictive power of the model.

3.8 Conclusion

Except for poverty, Carter's five factors appear to be significant indicators of terrorist attacks. This successfully answers the first question posed in Section 1.3. However, it is important to note that this model lacks predictive power, as the predictions have a large error range Therefore, it is now important to answer the other research questions and explore or further examine new and existing factors and their potential relationships with the number of terrorist attacks in Chapter 4. This analysis seeks greater insight into terrorism in Africa yielding a more accurate predictive model.

IV. Exploratory Analysis

4.1 Overview

This chapter answers the second proposed research question from Section 1.3:

- Can other potential indicators of terrorism be quantitatively explored and supported with a generalized linear model?

Similar to Chapter III, data collection and data treatment are conducted. The scope, assumptions, and methodology remain the same for this analysis in order to maintain consistency. Next, the analysis is conducted including a time blocked cross-validation to measure predictive power.

4.2 Data Collection

To explore other potential indicators of terrorism, data that accurately describes these indicators are found and aggregated. This section details the selected indicators, the chosen proxy variables, and their data sources. As described in Section 3.3, the missing data are filled using the k-nearest neighbors imputation method and then the independent data are mean-corrected and standardized.

Population.

A survey paper written by Krieger and Meierrieks [34] found fourteen articles that found a positive relationship between population and terrorist attacks. No other relationship in the survey paper had more articles in agreement than the positive relationship between population and terrorism. Some of these articles suggested that population be included in any analysis to control for the effect of population upon the number of attacks. Population statistics come from the World Bank database.

Population Density.

In Section 2.3, the indicators that the Department of Homeland Security uses as indicators of terrorism are discussed. One of these indicators is population density, since there is the desire to conduct attacks on these concentrated target centers. Consequently, this indicator is included to evaluate how well population density serves as an indicator of terrorism. Population density statistics come from the World Bank database and are the average number of people per square kilometer of land in the country.

Unemployment.

Another commonly researched indicator is unemployment, however, many articles come to conflicting conclusions regarding the statistic. One potential reason for these disparate results is different data sources with different definitions of unemployment. In numerous databases, individual countries define unemployment differently. These different definitions cause the countries to be compared to each other based upon different scales. To remedy this problem, the unemployment data are projections from the International Labor Organization, which uses one common definition and evaluates across the entire world. The data comes from the World Bank database and is recorded as the percentage of people unemployed in the country.

There is a difference between unemployed and underemployed, where the latter are individuals working at a level where they are drastically overqualified. Data representing underemployment were not accessible through direct or indirect means where the integrity of the data was consistent with the rest of the variables. However, in future research, it would be interesting to explore the relationship between underemployment and terrorism, if reputable data could be collected.

Military Expenditure.

In terrorism research, it is common to analyze the level of democracy or the type of government. One common problem with these analyses is that the level of democracy is a subjective measure or the type of government can be drastically different when comparing the official type of government with the subjective opinion of how the country is actually governed. In Li's analysis, the level of democracy is broken into constituent parts and analyzed to determine the effect of democracy through the constituent parts [29]. Another important aspect of government is the importance of the military. In order to assess the importance of the military to the government, the percentage of GDP spent on the military is assessed. This data comes from the World Bank database.

Education Expenditure.

Another important aspect of the government and a commonly debated indicator in terrorism research is education. In order to gauge the level and importance of education in a country, the percentage of GDP spent on education is assessed. The data comes from the World Bank database.

Urbanization.

In Section 2.3, modern terrorists are shown to both hide and conduct their operations in cities. Therefore, it follows that countries with higher levels of urbanization could potentially have more terrorist attacks. In order to analyze this belief, the level of urbanization in a country is analyzed. The data comes from the World Bank database and is the percentage of people living in urban areas.

Life Expectancy.

Life expectancy is the average age a newborn infant would live if prevailing patterns at the time of birth were to remain constant throughout its life and can serve as an indicator of the conditions in a country, such as medical, sanitary, and security. The relation, if any, to terrorism is explored. The data comes from the World Bank database.

Gender Equality.

How a country treats women and the opportunities that women have can be very descriptive. To analyze the relationship with terrorism, an indicator of gender equality is included in the model. This indicator is the ratio of girls to boys enrolled in secondary education and comes from the World Bank database. Data addressing the population gender ratio or the gender ratio in the work place would be interesting to analyze for future analysis. However, analyzing the ratio in secondary education shows more than the number of females to males, but also addresses women's rights, especially education, in these countries. Consequently, this metric will be used to assess gender equality.

Freedom of the Press.

Since the GTD's data collection process uses open media sources to find terrorist attacks, a Freedom of the Press index is used to control for countries with closed media sources. The index used comes from Freedom House, which is the same source used by Drakos and Li [30, 29].

Foreign Intervention.

It is interesting to look at the relationship between foreign intervention and terrorist attacks as well. The data for foreign intervention is a sub-indicator from the Fragile State Index called external intervention. External intervention is defined as the effect of other countries upon the country of interest.

Oil Production.

Our review of the literature determined that oil production has not been analyzed with regards to terrorism. While not applicable to the whole world, this variable could highlight a relationship specific to the African continent. This data for this indicator comes from U.S. Department of Energy and looks at total annual oil production in average thousand barrels per day.

Carter's Factors.

Also included in this model are four of five of the factors analyzed in Chapter three. The four factors include economic fragility, lack of border control, political corruption, and social fragmentation. Poverty was not included in this model due to the data imputation, since poverty had the most missing data points of any other variable, almost 80%. Furthermore, this variable was found to be insignificant in both the Chapter III model, as well as other research in the field [34]. Additionally, research specific to finding the relationship between poverty and terrorism has already been thoroughly conducted. The results are that poverty and terrorism do not have a strong relationship. Lastly, in a practical sense, witholding poverty from the model reduces the amount of data necessary to conduct the analysis, which allows an additional variable to be analyzed.

Contagion.

Lastly, contagion is well founded in the terrorism literature [34, 1]. Contagion is an autoregressive component, specifically a lag term. Most articles only analyze one lag of the dependent variable, but this research analyzes two lags of the dependent variable. These lag terms are simply the number of terrorist attacks in the same country from the previous year or two. In order to maintain consistency, this data comes from the GTD.

4.3 Results

In order to find robust, accurate, and predictive indicators of terrorism, multiple iterations of model construction were undertaken. The following sections report the model, block cross-validation, and the reasoning for constructing the model. Then a comparison of the models is conducted.

Full Model and Blocked Cross-Validation.

The results of the full model can be seen in Table 8.

At $\alpha = .05$, unemployment, freedom of the press and the two year lag are significant, with freedom of the press having a negative relationship. Other research commonly finds a positive relationship between terrorism and freedom of the press due to the data collection process, however, this research analyzed the whole world and start analysis in 1968. In Africa since 2007, freedom of the press allows citizens to express their political disdain through other means than terrorism, so the presence of freedom of the press indicates less terrorism. At $\alpha = .01$, population, education expenditure, life expectancy, gender equality, foreign intervention, fragmentation, and the one year lag are all significant with gender equality exhibiting a negative relationship and the largest absolute effect on terrorism. Consequently, countries providing

Table 8. Comparison of Models using All Variables

	Dependent variable:	
	Terrorist Attacks	
	Full Model	Full Model without outliers
Population	0.498***	0.420***
	(0.124)	(0.108)
Population.Density	0.087	0.216
	(0.147)	(0.152)
Unemployment	0.350**	0.376***
	(0.139)	(0.142)
Military	−0.109	−0.223*
	(0.117)	(0.124)
Education	0.750***	0.650***
	(0.140)	(0.146)
Urbanization	0.199	0.204
	(0.134)	(0.138)
Life.Expectancy	0.539***	0.407***
	(0.129)	(0.140)
Gender.Equality	−0.793***	−0.764***
	(0.135)	(0.138)
Freedom.of.the.Press	−0.297**	−0.279**
	(0.123)	(0.125)
Foreign.Intervention	0.687***	0.557***
	(0.153)	(0.151)
EVI	−0.078	−0.122
	(0.119)	(0.120)
Border.Security	0.187	0.250*
	(0.146)	(0.151)
Fragmentation	0.606***	0.519***
	(0.150)	(0.150)
Corruption	0.013	0.001
	(0.143)	(0.139)
Oil.Production	0.098	0.047
	(0.139)	(0.139)
One.yr.lag	0.478***	0.835***
	(0.156)	(0.175)
Two.yr.lag	0.396**	0.018
	(0.157)	(0.178)

Note: *p<0.1; **p<0.05; ***p<0.01

Table 9. Comparison of Blocked Cross-Validation Results across models

	2008 SSE	2009 SSE	2010 SSE	2011 SSE	2012 SSE	2013 SSE	Total CV RMSE	CV RMSE without 2013
Full Model	N/A	N/A	57412161.0	347940.5	9922063.0	40924770000000.0	456946.6	678.54
Full Model without outliers	N/A	N/A	6354.3	6728.9	7931.3	152853.5	30.4	12.21
Reduced Model	N/A	139910592	6832551.0	615862.8	12216125.0	15834960000000.0	232079.6	807.05
Reduced Model without outliers	2925.2	5456.5	4607.9	4139.9	7879.5	151084.3	25.0	10.32

secondary education opportunities to women seem able to decrease terrorism more than if that country had high border security or greater military expenditure.

In Table 12, the blocked cross-validation results can be seen for all of the models. Each variable has the parameter estimate, the variance below the estimate, and rotation depicting significance level. Clearly, this model lacks predictive capability. First, due to the data requirements of the IRLS algorithm to approximate theta, which is based upon the number of variables in the independent data, the models for 2008 and 2009 could not be constructed. Second, validation residuals are high due to misfitting the model. The model predicting 2013 attacks (using 2007-2012 data) predicts 6.4 million terrorist attacks for Nigeria and over 17 thousand for Somalia. Since the highest number of attacks in the dataset is 597 (Nigeria 2012), these estimates drastically increase the error term. Before conducting any analysis, the countries of Nigeria and Somalia were considered outliers in regards to the dependent variable. These two countries represent the top 5% of terrorist attacks on average for Africa in this time period, which can be seen in Figure 4.

Being in the top 5% does not make them outliers by themselves, however, their averages of 202 attacks for Somalia and 194 attacks for Nigeria grossly outweigh Algeria, the country with the third largest average of 74 attacks. These countries are clearly outliers in terrorist attacks and essentially leverage the model parameters to

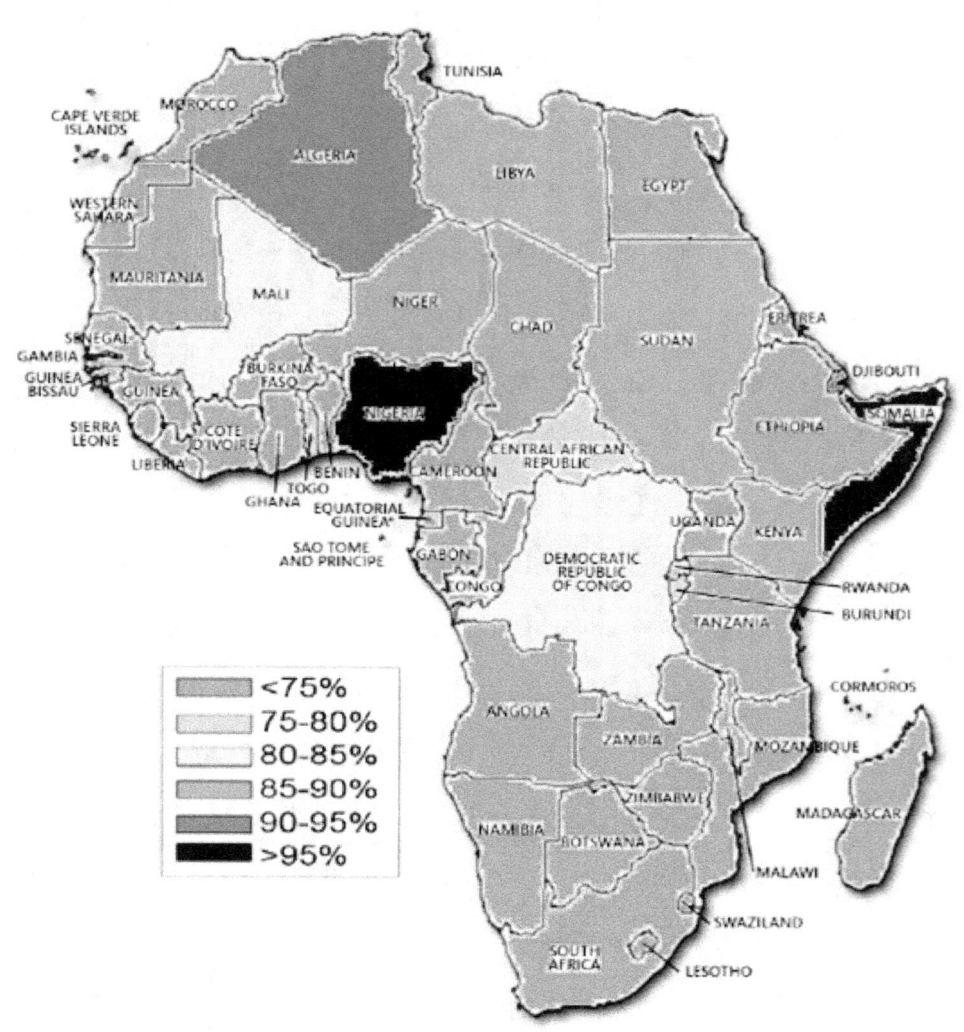

Figure 4. Cumulative Distribution of African Countries by 2007-2013 Average Annual Terrorist Attacks

get the best fits. In order to remedy this problem, these countries are removed from the model and the model is rerun. While it is undesirable to remove countries from the model, it is the interest of this research to determine the relationships between terrorism throughout all of Africa and these indicators, not only Nigeria and Somalia. Additionally, this model should help countries predict the extent of their vulnerability to terrorism in order to prepare for the attacks. Countries like Somalia and Nigeria can expect consistently large amount of terrorist attacks at least in the near future. Therefore, removing Somalia and Nigeria from the model does not compromise the main purpose of the model.

Full Model with Nigeria and Somalia removed and Blocked Cross-Validation.

The results of the full model with Nigeria and Somalia removed can be seen in the left column of Table 8. Removing outliers caused border security and military expenditure to become significant in the model with $\alpha = .10$, where military expenditure has a negative relationship with terrorism. Additionally, the removal of outliers causes the two year lag to no longer be significant and almost doubles the effect of the one year lag causing it to be the greatest indicator of terrorism incidents. This indicates the level of activity seen in the previous year is likely to continue. Lastly, unemployment became significant at $\alpha = .01$.

In Table 12, the blocked cross-validation results can be seen for all of the models. This model clearly outperforms the full model in regards to predictive capability. The root mean square error (RMSE) of approximately 30 indicates that predictions are likely to be within 30 incidents. Without considering the year 2013, the model has an RMSE of approximately 12 incidents. Thirty incidents, while much smaller than the full model, is still a very wide range for predicting terrorist attacks, especially considering the effects of one terrorist attack. Consequently, it was decided to conduct a backward stepwise regression based upon AIC to construct the model and then validate the smaller model.

Reduced Model and Blocked Cross-Validation.

Using a stepwise regression that minimizes AIC, a reduced model is constructed. The reduced model can be seen in Table 10. Unemployment, urbanization, freedom of the press, and the two year lag are significant at $\alpha = .05$ with freedom of the press maintaining a negative relationship. All of the variables that are significant at $\alpha = .01$ in the full model are still significant at that level, with gender equality having a negative relationship with the largest absolute relationship with terrorism.

One particular variable that was not included in the analysis was a spatial component, or analyzing the terrorism occurring in neighboring countries. Looking at Figure 4 the countries with more terrorist attacks tend to border each other. In order to assess if this is true, a variable that measures the spatial component is constructed. This variable was constructed similarly to border security, but used one year lag values instead of the security apparatus score. The number of attacks that occurred in neighboring countries is multiplied by the percentage of border shared with that country. Then, these numbers are aggregated for all of the bordering countries of the focal country. This variable is essentially a spatial autoregressive component and is added to the reduced model with the results in Table 11.

In Table 12, the blocked cross-validation results can be seen for all of the models. This model performs poorly in terms of prediction for the same reason behind the poor performance of the full model with outliers. This model has fewer indicators, which means that fewer indicators have to be monitored in the future. Additionally, the smaller dimensionality of the problem allowed blocked cross-validation to be conducted for every year.

Table 10. Comparison of Models using stepwise process

	Dependent variable:	
	Terrorist Attacks	
	Reduced Model	Reduced Model without outliers
Population	0.562***	0.439***
	(0.101)	(0.101)
Unemployment	0.261**	0.289**
	(0.128)	(0.117)
Education	0.728***	0.606***
	(0.132)	(0.132)
Urbanization	0.255**	
	(0.119)	
Life.Expectancy	0.550***	0.474***
	(0.124)	(0.128)
Gender.Equality	−0.802***	−0.710***
	(0.130)	(0.133)
Freedom.of.the.Press	−0.290**	−0.229**
	(0.117)	(0.117)
Foreign.Intervention	0.651***	0.417***
	(0.131)	(0.133)
Border.Security		0.247*
		(0.139)
Fragmentation	0.687***	0.528***
	(0.135)	(0.135)
One.yr.lag	0.511***	0.739***
	(0.155)	(0.093)
Two.yr.lag	0.371**	
	(0.153)	
Constant	0.848***	0.556***
	(0.101)	(0.103)
Note:		*p<0.1; **p<0.05; ***p<0.01

Reduced Model with Nigeria and Somalia removed and Blocked Cross-Validation.

Conducting a separate stepwise regression minimizing AIC created the reduced model with the outliers, Nigeria and Somalia, removed can be seen in Table 10. Compared to the reduced model with outliers, urbanization and the two year lag are no longer significant at $\alpha = .10$. This makes sense since these countries have had sustained terrorism problems and Nigeria has the greatest amount of urbanization due to the only mega-city in Africa, Lagos. Furthermore, border security became significant at $\alpha = .10$, which shows that border security is an important indicator of terrorism in Africa excluding Somalia and Nigeria. Otherwise all other indicators maintain the same significance level and relationship direction. However, the actual parameter estimates do change causing the one year lag to have the greatest relationship with terrorism.

Similar to the previous model, a spatial autoregressive component is added to the reduced model with the results in Table 11.

In Table 12, the blocked cross-validation results are summarized for all of the models. This model performs better than any other model. The total RMSE is approximately 25 incidents and approximately 10 without the year 2013. Furthermore, this model has fewer indicators, which means that fewer indicators have to be monitored in the future. Additionally, the smaller dimensionality of the problem allowed conducting blocked cross-validation for every year.

Model Comparisons.

It is worth discussing the poor predictive performance of the year 2013 models. All of the models grossly miss predicted the number of terrorist attacks in the year 2013 during blocked cross-validation. It is important to note that 2013 saw a drastic increase in terrorism across much of Africa. Djibouti recorded 196 more attacks than the previous 6 years combined. Libya recorded 173 more attacks than the previous 6 years combined and Mozambique recorded 14 more attacks than the previous 6 years combined. This sharp increase in attacks shows the growing problem of terrorism throughout Africa. Additionally, it shows that the year 2013 stands out in comparison to the other years in the model due to the much larger scale of terrorism. It is believed this 2013 increase changed the semi-stationary temporal nature of the incidents; meaning the variance in the incidents was too great for this model to predict accurately.

In order to assess why the model does not capture the drastic changes in 2013, the reduced model without outliers predictions for 2013 is examined. A map of the predictions by this model can be seen in Figure 5.

Only three countries had predictions off by more than 60 (Djibouti, Libya, and Kenya) and 90% of countries fell within the RMSE of 25 attacks. Djibouti had 263 attacks more than predicted. While the model predicted a slight increase from the previous, it did not capture the extent of the increase. It is believed that this changed occurred due to increased foreign military presence, especially by the United States. The model predicted a doubling of the attacks from 2012 for Libya, but it was still under predicted by 195 attacks. It is believed this occurred due to the change in government with the removal of Gaddafi. Kenya's number of attacks for 2013 stayed the same, but the model predicted 191 more attacks. When looking at the data, a lot of indicators changed slightly indicating more attacks. These slight increases when aggregated vastly over-estimated the 2013 prediction. It is believed more data would have prevented this problem by fine-tuning the data. In conclusion, this model can still be improved upon. A predictive model that is off by approximately 25 attacks is better than no model, but has a large amount of variability to make

65

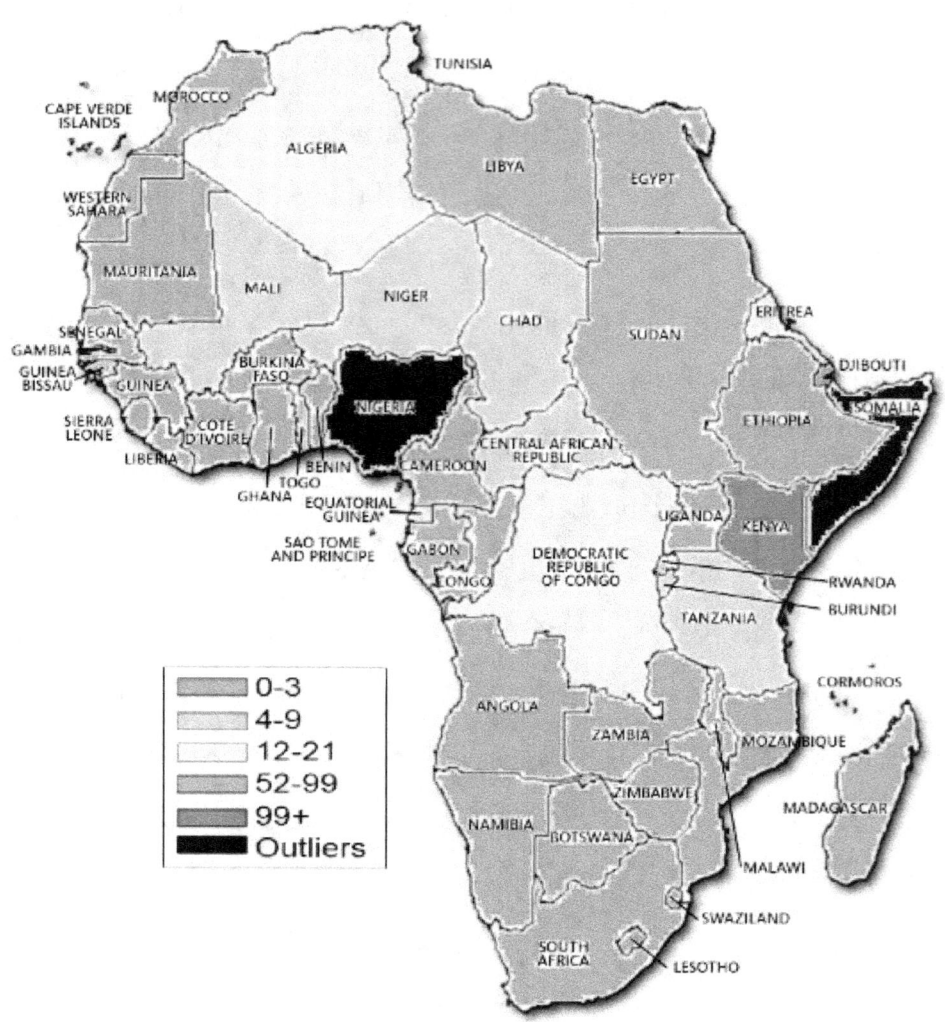

Figure 5. 2013 Model Predictions for Reduced Model without Outliers

Table 11. Comparison of All Models Including Spatial Component

	AIC	BIC	Number of Variables	Total CV RMSE	CV RMSE without 2013
Carter Model (poverty removed)	1605.09	1628.11	4	50.12	42.07
Full Model	1482.93	1555.85	17	456946.60	678.54
Full Model without outlier	1267.41	1339.53	17	30.41	12.21
Reduced Model	1473.53	1523.42	11	232079.62	807.05
Reduced Model without outliers	1258.43	1303.99	10	24.99	10.32
Reduced Model (with Spatial)	1475.27	1529.00	12	254337.10	2419.63
Reduced Model without outliers (Spatial)	1260.04	1309.39	11	24.16	11.22

practical decisions. Consequently, in future research it is recommended to include foreign military presence, changes in government, and include more terrorism data as it becomes available.

In Table 11, the different attributes of the models are compared. As mentioned previously the reduced model without Nigeria and Somalia outperformed the other models in predictive capability and dimensionality. Additionally, reduced model without Nigeria and Somalia outperformed the other models in regards to AIC and BIC. Furthermore, a likelihood-ratio test, which is discussed in Section 2.5, between the models without outliers indicate that the reduced model is superior with a p-value of .540. It is also interesting to note that reduced model without outliers improves the model fit and cuts the RMSE in half when compared to the best model from the confirmatory analysis.

The fit of the model and the cross-validation RMSE without 2013 perform slightly worse with the addition of the spatial component. Additionally, the spatial component is not statistically significant when added to the reduced model with or without outliers. However, the addition of the spatial component does improve the overall cross-validation results. In order to analyze what is occurring. The SSE for the time-blocked cross-validation can be seen in Table 12.

Table 12. Comparison of All Models by Cross-Validation Including Spatial Component

	2008 SSE	2009 SSE	2010 SSE	2011 SSE	2012 SSE	2013 SSE	Total CV RMSE	CV RMSE without 2013
Full Model	N/A	N/A	57412161.0	347940.5	9922063.0	40924770000000.0	456946.6	678.54
Full Model without outliers	N/A	N/A	6354.3	6728.9	7931.3	152853.5	30.4	12.21
Reduced Model	N/A	139910592	6832551.0	615862.8	12216125.0	15834960000000.0	232079.6	807.05
Reduced Model without outliers	2925.2	5456.5	4607.9	4139.9	7879.5	151084.3	25.0	10.32
Reduced Model Spatial	N/A	1.093E+09	23911670.0	1766888.0	28477586.0	15847260000000.0	254337.10	2419.63
Reduced Model without outliers (Spatial)	3115.3	3153.3	11471.7	4567.5	7299.2	135034.2	24.16	11.22

It appears that including the spatial component makes predictions worse for 2008, 201,0 and 2011, the best years of prediction for the reduced model without outliers. However, it predicts much better in 2012 and 2013, which are the worst predictions for the reduced model without outliers. Therefore, it appears that the spatial component is growing in importance as an indicator. This can be seen by comparing the average number of attacks for the entire data set (Figure 4) and the predictions for 2013 (Figure 5).

It is believed that there is not enough modern data to cause the spatial component to be significant. However, when more data is available, adding this component to future analysis would likely improve predictive capability and especially address the worse predictions in recent years.

4.4 Conclusion

The reduced model removing outliers performs best compared to the other models. The variables population, education, life expectancy, gender equality, foreign intervention, fragmentation, and the one year lag have a robust relationship with terrorism. This model answers the second research question. To answer the third research question, these relationships are analyzed using classification.

V. Classification

5.1 Overview

The third and final research question proposed in Section 1.3:

- Can these variable relationships undergo classification methods, such as classification trees, in order to determine breakpoints in socio-economic characteristics of countries, which indicate increased vulnerability to terror attacks?

To answer this question, classification trees are constructed and analyzed. Classification trees are used to analyze the newly found indicator relationships and to determine breakpoints of these relationships that indicate either an increase or decrease vulnerability to terrorism.

5.2 Classes

To conduct classification, the dependent data is divided into classes. The purpose of this classification is to determine which countries are most vulnerable to terrorism and which factors (at specific levels) these countries have in common. While it is true that one terrorist attack can have severe consequences, one terrorist attack could be labeled as a terrorist incident rather than a recurring problem. Therefore, the cutoff will not be countries with no attacks and countries with one or more attacks. Additionally, by not using one as the cutoff, this provides a buffer against common complaints against the GTD such as data collection and a broad definition of terrorism. Classification trees require sufficient observations in both classes so that insight can be provided for both sides of the tree. This is due to the nature of classification trees and their dependence upon sample size. Table 13 depicts cumulative probability of number of attacks.

Table 13. Distribution of Terrorist Attacks

Number of Attacks	Number of Observations	% of Attacks	Cumulative % of Attacks
0	177	52%	52%
1	44	13%	64%
2	19	6%	70%
3	15	4%	74%
4	10	3%	77%
5	6	2%	79%
6	5	1%	80%
7	4	1%	82%
>7	63	18%	100%

The cutoff was set to four terrorist attacks. This means that countries with less than four attacks in a year are in one class and those with four or more attacks are in the other class. This allows the focus on terrorism to highlight the top 25% of annual terrorist attacks. This classification looks at socio-economic indicators and the breakpoints of those indicators which separate the top 25% of annual terrorist attacks.

5.3   Classification Tree Description

Classification Trees analyze a relationship between variables. As opposed to regression, classification trees analyze the independent variables in regards to a dependent variable which split the data into classes. The independent variable that causes the greatest split in the dependent data starts the tree. For instance, all or the vast majority of countries with a population greater than some amount are more likely to have a higher vulnerability to terrorism. Conversely, countries below the same specified population are less vulnerable to terrorism. This divides the data into two groups. Using the same procedure, these groups are further split using factors which provide the best classification potential. This continues until a group can no longer

71

be split or some other stopping criteria is met. At the end of each branch of the tree is a number that represents the dominant class at the end of that branch. ANOVA trees differ from classification trees in that instead of classes they divide the data into larger and smaller values and report the average at the end of the tree. When using a zero or one as the values of the dependent variable, an ANOVA tree returns the percentage of the group in class one. Therefore, in order to add transparency, ANOVA results using the class dependent variable are added to the classification trees.

To interpret a classification tree, an individual, or in this case a country, assess which side of the breakpoint they lie upon and follow that branch. Then they would do the same at the next breakpoint until they reach the end of the tree. At the end of the tree they should determine whether they were correctly classified, determine their prediction for the upcoming year, or look at attributes of similar countries in the other class depending upon their purposes for using the tree.

5.4 Models

Two different models are used to construct classification trees. The first tree is constructed using all the variables from the full model of the exploratory analysis. The second model only looks at the variables used in the reduced model without outliers. The lags are left out of the classification since the goal of this research is to find indicators which could be used to decrease terrorism vulnerability. Finding the breakpoints in the lags does not provide useful insight as they are not directly controllable. Additionally, while some models removed the countries of Nigeria and Somalia from analysis, these countries remain in the analysis of classification trees. Due to classification, the extent of terrorism in these countries no longer drives the model, but are simply grouped in with the other country-year combinations with four or more attacks. The class with less than four attacks is represented by a 0 and the class with four or more attacks is represented with a 1.

Full Model Classification.

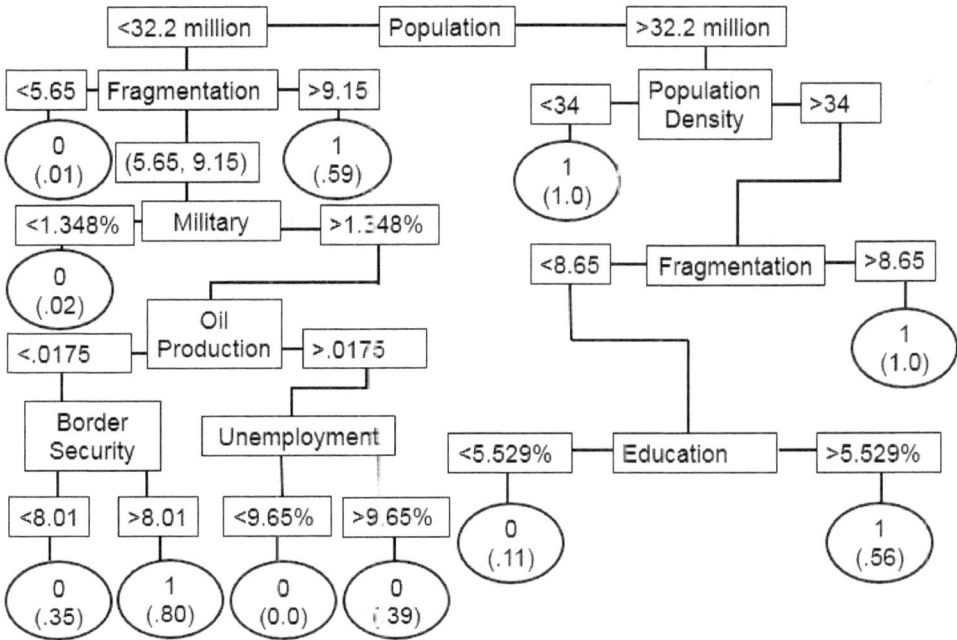

Figure 6. Classification Tree for Full Model

The classification tree for the full model can be seen in Figure 6. Circles at the end of the tree indicate the classification, either a 0 or 1, and the ANOVA results in parentheses show the percentage of data points in the group of class 1, high vulnerability. The first division in the tree comes from population with the breaking point at approximately 32.2 million people. The greatest separation occurs where the country population is greater than 32.2 million (right side of the tree).

Continuing on the right branch of the tree the next division is population density at 34 people per square kilometer. Based upon our sample, when a country's population is higher than 32.2 million and population density is less than 34 people per square kilometer that country is likely to experience 4 or more terrorist attacks. If the population density is greater than 34, the tree continues down to the fragmentation score. A fragmentation score at this point greater than 8.65 always resulted in four or more attacks in our example, where as less than that score resulted in analyzing education. The education cutoff is 5.529 where countries spending more than 5.529% of GDP on education are more likely to have a terrorist problem. However, unlike the previously discussed classifications, the ANOVA results show that this cutoff is not definite and contains some misclassification.

If the country has less than 32.2 million people, then fragmentation is the next indicator to monitor. A fragmentation score higher than 9.15 makes terrorism more likely, but not definite. However, a fragmentation score lower than 5.65 means the vulnerability of a terrorism problem is likely small. If the fragmentation score is between these ranges than the percent of GDP spent on the military is the next indicator to examine. A country spending less than 1.348% is less likely to have a terrorist problem, while other countries need to examine annual oil production. If oil production is greater than .0175, regardless of the unemployment level resulted in low vulnerability. Misclassification was at 38% for unemployment exceeding 9.65%; this means oil producing countries with higher unemployment are more vulnerable. Countries with oil production lower than .0175, next need to address border security. Countries with border security greater than 8, at this point in the tree, have greater vulnerability. While countries with a border security less than 8 only had less terrorism vulnerability.

Now that this tree has been constructed, it is important to analyze these findings to determine intervention strategies. It is not surprising that population is the first classifier, since it is the most robust indicator in terrorism research. However, population size cannot be easily influenced. Other variables of note include fragmentation and population density, but once again not much can be done to influence these indicators. However, countries with less than 32.2 million people with fragmentation scores less than 9.15 have some options to reduce the chances of high vulnerability to a terrorism threat. These options include spending less on the military, however, this could be ill-advised. If a country is an oil producer, it should focus on having a low unemployment rate. This makes sense since oil producing countries are likely to have better finances and a large unemployed population within that country is likely to be disgruntled and potentially look to terrorism for either political dissonance or to receive some money. If the country does not produce much oil, it is wise for that country to invest in border security, because this could potentially reduce terrorism.

It is interesting to note that many of the variables deemed unimportant in regression become classifiers in the classification tree. This does not attack the legitimacy of either methodology, but means that variables for predicting the quantity of terrorist attacks and the variables for splitting high and low numbers of attacks are different. In order to assess how well classification works for the variables in model 3, another classification tree is constructed.

Reduced Model Classification.

The classification tree for the reduced model can be seen in Figure 7. Consistent with the full model, population is the first classifier with a breakpoint at 32.2 million people. Those with populations greater 32.2 million then need to assess their fragmentation score. 19 out of 20 countries with fragmentation scores higher than 8.05 have high vulnerability, while other countries must assess their level of foreign intervention. All countries with foreign intervention scores greater than 8.55 at this point have a terrorism problem, while other countries need to assess the urbanization of their population. Those countries with an urban population greater than 62.48%, are more likely to have a terrorist problem than those that do not.

Those countries with a population less than 32.2 million also need to assess their

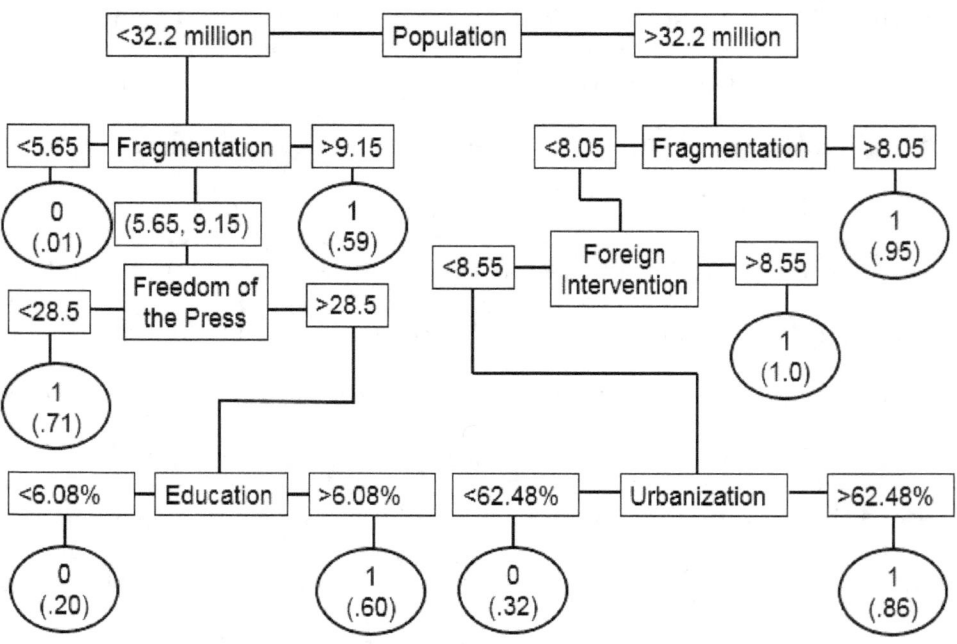

Figure 7. Classification Tree for Reduced Model

fragmentation score. Countries with a fragmentation score greater than 9.15 are more likely to have a terrorist problem, while countries with a fragmentation score less than 5.65 are considered to have low terrorism vulnerability. The countries who's fragmentation falls between these intervals need to evaluate their freedom of the press. Countries with a low freedom of the press, less than 28.5, are more vulnerable, while the other country outcomes are based upon their education spending. Countries spending greater than 6.082% of their GDP on education are more likely to have a terrorism problem than countries which spend less.

This model has many similarities to the other model, such as population and fragmentation being very important to classifying. However, there are numerous differences as well. The indicators of foreign intervention, urbanization, education, and freedom of the press are now useful classifiers and much easier to influence than the population and fragmentation in a country. Consequently, the governing body of the country has more feasible options to mitigate their country is terrorism vulnerability. For instance, countries with large populations and low fragmentation scores can decrease the terrorism threat by decreasing foreign intervention or at least the perception, decrease urbanization by encouraging suburban living, and decreasing spending on education or decrease the connection between general education and changes to culture and society which perpetrates a terrorist mindset. On the other hand, countries with populations less than 32.2 million and with fragmentation scores between 5.65 and 9.15 can increase the freedom of the press in their country and decreasing spending on education or decrease the connection between general education and societal changes which harbor a terrorist mindset. Coupling these strategies with the strategies from the other classification tree provides leaders with a better understanding of terrorists and some potential ways to decrease the vulnerability to terrorism in countries across Africa.

5.5 Conclusion

Now that numerous indicators have been quantitatively explored, greater insight has been found into terrorism and the terrorist mindset. These indicators have been explored and have confirmed already found relationships, determined new previously unexplored relationships, and confirmed non-existent relationships. Furthermore, these indicators have been further examined using classification and certain breakpoints have been identified which can be used to determine the attributes of countries with greater terrorism threats, defined as the countries with the upper quartile in annual terrorist attacks. While population and fragmentation in a country are the main indicators of a terrorism problem, other indicators that can be influenced or shaped within the constraints of the government were also found to reduce the effects of terrorism vulnerability. These variables include military expenditure, border security, unemployment, freedom of the press, urbanization, education, and foreign intervention. Lastly, these breakpoints were analyzed to give recommendations to decision makers and the governing bodies of each country.

VI. Conclusion

6.1 Summary

Currently, the U.S. government lacks a thorough knowledge of terrorism and their mindsets, which causes the U.S. to take a reactionary response to terrorism instead of a preventative approach. This research provided an outline to test social science perspectives on terrorism and gain greater strategic insights into terrorism in Africa.

These questions were answered in Chapters III, IV, & V, respectively. The first question looked to statistically defend the qualitatively based findings of Carter. The second question examined additional variables beyond these explained by Carter. The third question involved assessing important variables using a classification tree to determine the breakpoints of these indicators.

6.2 Key Findings

The answer to these research questions returned numerous results; the key results are summarized below.

Confirmatory Analysis.

Of Carter's five factors, four of them were found statistically significant. Poverty was insignificant, a common finding among terrorism research. Of the four significant variables, only economic vulnerability had a relationship with terrorism contrary to Carter's beliefs. Economic fragility seems to indicate less terrorist attacks, since stable economies provide preferred targets for terrorism. The last three variables were corruption, border security, and fragmentation. In terrorism research, this is the first time that border security has been assessed and a proxy defining the relationship of greater border security is used. Results show a reduction in terrorist attacks where border security is greater.

Additionally, fragmentation held the greatest significance in the model and was the second most important variable in classification after population, a common and well defined indicator of terrorism in the literature. Carter's qualitative analysis did not perform well after being quantitatively assessed, however, not all of her five factors were significant and the blocked cross-validation results produced a RMSE greater than 50. Clearly, Carter's five factors were not all related to terrorism and they are not adequate by themselves to closely predict the number of terrorist attacks. Consequently, an exploratory analysis of additional indicators garnered insight about terrorism and helped to construct a potential preventative strategy.

Exploratory Analysis.

In the exploratory analysis, 17 potential indicators of terrorism, including the four significant factors from Carter's research were included. While some expected relationships were robustly significant, such as population and fragmentation, other unexpected relationships were robustly significant, such as education spending and gender equality. Additionally, gender equality had the largest effect on terrorism, behind the one year lag. The inclusion of these additional variables eventually led to a model with a RMSE of approximately 25, reducing the confirmatory analysis results by half.

Classification Analysis.

In order to further explore these variable relationships, the same variables were used for classification purposes. A classification tree was used to determine the break-points of these variables in order to determine the characteristics of countries with

Table 14. Top Indicators Across All Analyses

	Confirmatory	Exploratory	Classification
Economic Fragility	X		
Border Security	X	X	X
Corruption	X		
Fragmentation	X	X	X
Population		X	X
Population Density			X
Unemployment		X	X
Military Expenditure			X
Education Expenditure		X	X
Urbanization			X
Life Expectancy		X	
Gender Equality		X	
Freedom of the Press		X	X
Foreign Intervention		X	X
Oil Production			X
One Year Lag		X	
Two Year Lag			

and without a terrorism problem. It is important to note that a terrorism problem is defined as having four or more attacks in a year. Two trees were constructed using either 15 of the potential indicators, lag terms were excluded, or the 8 indicators that were determined important. Both of these trees showed the importance of population of and fragmentation in a country to the number of terrorist attacks. Although these indicators are not easily changed, other indicators were also found to be significant that can be altered much easier. This could lead to anti-terrorism strategies specific to a country at certain population and fragmentation levels.

Overall.

Table 14 provides a summary of the analyses outcomes for all three approaches. An "X" in the column represents either significance in the best model or presence(as in the classification trees). Border Security and Fragmentation are the most robust indicators since they are important in all three analyses. Population, Unemployment, Education Expenditure, Freedom of the Press, Foreign Intervention, and the One Year Lag are also considered robust indicators, since they were deemed important in every model they were analyzed.

6.3   Contributions

This research contains numerous implications and contributions to the academic field of terrorism research as well as a practical approach to the governments confronting terrorism that were not found in the extensive literature review conducted for this research.

Academic Contributions.

This research is scoped to focus on recent terrorism threats in a specific region. It is the first time where Africa has been exclusively examined with regards to terrorism. While other researchers have used indicator variables to represent Africa, exclusively examining Africa provides a clarity for how the specific variables operate for this continent. Additionally, many researchers use as much data as possible going back to the late 60's. However, due to the changing nature of terrorism, this is the first research to capture modern terrorism by examining the terrorism from the years 2007 to 2013.

The next academic contributions come from the confirmatory analysis. This is the first time that a qualitative article has been examined and analyzed to provide quantitative support. Conducting this type of exploratory analysis, provides support or helps to counter perceived observational findings or initial beliefs about terrorism. Second, many of the variables were seldom examined. Specific proxies for qualitative concepts are identified and investigated. Poverty and economic fragility specifically incorporated new proxies, with less literature findings. Additionally, border security remained a qualitative before. Now this research confirms the belief that greater border security reduces terrorism, quantitatively. This shows the importance of bridging inter-discipline gaps among qualitative and quantitative research.

The rest of the academic contributions come from the exploratory analysis. As mentioned before, this research is a new attempt to exclusively analyze Africa in regards to terrorist attacks. Consequently, investigating variables which hold unique meaning for Africa. Oil production is one variable that has rarely been analyzed before and was found to have no statistically significant effect on the number of terrorist attacks in Africa. Additionally, robustly significant relationships were found for population, education spending, gender equality, and fragmentation. While it is very common to build a model to examine relationships in the literature, it is rare to test the predictive capabilities of the model. Next, the variables from the exploratory analysis were used to construct classification trees to further analyze the relationships and develop potential courses of action. This type of analysis is rarely done in terrorism research.

Practical Contributions.

Whenever conducting research it is important to consider who should care about this research and who would use this model. Clearly, African countries have a particular interest in the predictive model, as well as the classification trees, to reduce vulnerability to terrorism. Other countries, as well as international organizations who wish to reduce Africa's vulnerability to terrorism would also be interested in this research. In Africa, the Trans-Sahara Counter Terrorism Partnership, similar counter terrorism groups, and the African governments' specific counter terrorism or counter intelligence organizations could use this model to shape strategic decisions. Various U.S. organizations would have an interest in using this research including, AFRICOM and DHS. Lastly, other countries and international organizations with specific counter-terrorism components would find this research useful for considering future DIME operations.

This research also has numerous practical applications, especially for countries confronting terrorism. First, finding the statistically significant relationship between increasing border security and decreasing terrorism can be vital to anti-terrorism campaigns. While this finding may not at first seem impressive, it is important to note that no current strategy to reduce terrorism has been quantitatively supported [10]. Therefore, decision makers could look into spending money on border security across Africa which shows promise to reduce terrorism vulnerability; this translates to mitigating the terrorism threat and improving security stability across the region.

The other large practical application of this research are the potential strategies to reduce terrorism for countries with specific population sizes and fragmentation scores. Strategic resources put toward the right terrorism indicators provide a potential avenue to reduce the terrorism threat.

6.4   Future Research

While much research has been conducted to find the relationships indicative of terrorism, this task will never be completed. Additionally, few researchers have further explored these potential relationship and generated strategies to prevent terrorism. This leaves many areas for additional research, as well as adaptations to research.

Research Adaptations.

First, some changes could be made to the scope of the problem. For this research, it was decided to analyze Africa. Smaller or larger regions of the world could be analyzed. It may be interesting to see the effects of sub-Saharan Africa or parts of Africa that may have been colonized by a specific world power. In the opposite direction, it would be interesting to examine the same features including the Middle East or even on a global scale. This research has shown Africa specific relationships, such as border security, or lack of relationship, such as oil production. It would be interesting to test these relationships at the global level to see if they are valid only for Africa or descriptive of terrorism in general.

Another aspect of the scope that could be altered is the analysis time frame. Due to the establishment of AFRICOM and the Iraq troop surge, it was determined to start the analysis in the year 2007, however, claims could be made to analyze over other time periods. Once again, it would be interesting to take these results and see if they are applicable to other time frames. This would should how robust the results are and if our findings are applicable to pre-modern terrorism as well as modern terrorism.

Another important part of this research that could be adapted is variable selection. It would be interesting to analyze the results of the analysis, especially the exploratory analysis if different variables are selected. For instance, it was hoped that variables related to religion would be collected and analyzed, such as percent of the population that is Christian and the percent of the population that is Muslim. However, this data could not be collected with the same integrity as the other data used.

Additional Research.

Aside from potential adaptations, this research has set the foundation for future research to be conducted. First, further validation of the model should be competed with data that the GTD releases in 2015 and subsequent years. This could remedy problems with large miss predictions in 2013. Additionally, throughout the research, a shortage of data was a sizable concern. Having additional years provides more data for modern terrorism, which can be used to create an expanded model or to simply improve the current model.

The changes in 2013 indicate greater than expected increases. The models in this research, especially chapter III and IV, assume stationarity. This should be relaxed and methods developed or investigated to handle non-stationary time series data.

While not apparent in the 2013 data, a spatial component could be necessary to explain the sharp growth of terrorism in the year 2013 if this trend continues to 2014. Further improvements to the model could be pre-processing the data with a Principal Component Analysis (PCA). This could paint even more detail into how the independent data is interrelated and how those relationships affect terrorism. Additionally, discriminant analysis or neural networks could be used to classify aside from the classification tree in order to determine the important factors for classification by the size of affect as well as conducting a dimensionality assessment.

Additional research could be conducted to focus upon the practical application of this research. For instance, numerous strategies to potentially reduce terrorism vulnerability were highlighted. This strategy identifies which variables and their levels are indicators of terrorism. They do not describe specific strategies or actions required to help shape the environment. For instance, if a country needs to reduce unemployment, it could look at spending more on border security, which would provide additional jobs and further protect the borders. A greater understanding of the indicators will aid strategic decision making and resource allocation. Furthermore, these specific strategies should be examined or potentially simulated to determine their effects. For instance, it seems that promoting border security prevents terrorists from crossing the border and committing attacks, but does increased security stop the attack or just relegate it to the country of origin? This and similar questions should be answered before implementation. Once these questions are answered a risk analysis should be conducted upon these strategies to determine the worst case, best case, and most likely outcomes of the strategy. This additional analysis would bridge the gap between statistically validated suggestions and fully planned and implementable strategies.

6.5 Way Ahead

Since the late 90's, terrorism has been growing in both the quantity of terrorist attacks and the lethality of those attacks [3]. Various governments have witnessed this growing problem and responded with various counter-measures. With incidents in Africa at all time highs in 2013, these measures are proving inadequate. Identifying underlying patterns or indicators of terrorism provides an opportunity to change strategies and decisions to prevent greater escalation in the upcoming years. After years of conflict and military operations aimed at mitigating terrorism, we must look for ways to foster diplomatic relations and leverage other resources to reduce the vulnerability to terrorism across Africa and the World.

Bibliography

1. M. Gassebner and S. Luechinger, "Lock, stock, and barrel: A comprehensive assessment of the determinants of terror," *Public Choice*, vol. 149, no. 3-4, pp. 235–261, 2011.

2. D. Kilcullen, "Counter-insurgency redux," *Survival*, vol. 48, no. 4, pp. 111–130, 2006.

3. K. T. Bogen and E. D. Jones, "Risks of mortality and morbidity from worldwide terrorism: 1968–2004," *Risk Analysis*, vol. 26, no. 1, pp. 45–59, 2006.

4. B. Obama, "National strategy for counterterrorism," *Washington DC: White House, June*, 2011.

5. K. Gaibulloev and T. Sandler, "The adverse effect of transnational and domestic terrorism on growth in Africa," *Journal of Peace Research*, vol. 48, no. 3, pp. 355–371, 2011.

6. G. Mills and J. Herbst, "Africa, terrorism and AFRICOM," *The RUSI Journal*, vol. 152, no. 2, pp. 40–45, 2007.

7. R. Gates, "State department facts on country reports on terrorism 2013," 2014.

8. W. E. Gortney, "Joint publication 3–.07.2, antiterrorism." Department of Defense, November 2010.

9. W. Enders and T. Sandler, *The political economy of terrorism*. Cambridge University Press, 2011.

10. C. Lum, L. W. Kennedy, and A. Sherley, "Are counter-terrorism strategies effective? the results of the campbell systematic review on counter-terrorism evaluation research," *Journal of Experimental Criminology*, vol. 2, no. 4, pp. 489–516, 2006.

11. Study of Terrorism and Responses to Terrorism, "Codebook: Inclusion criteria and variables." START, August 2014. http://www.start.umd.edu/gtd/downloads/Codebook.pdf.

12. Y. Y. Haimes, "On the definition of vulnerabilities in measuring risks to infrastructures," *Risk Analysis*, vol. 26, no. 2, pp. 293–296, 2006.

13. R. Henry, "Department of Defense instruction 2000.16." Department of Defense, December 2006. http://www.dtic.mil/whs/directives/corres/pdf/200016p.pdf.

14. G. W. Bush, "National strategy for combating terrorism," *Washington DC: White House, June*, 2009.

15. R. Hillson, "The DIME/PMESII model suite requirements project," tech. rep., DTIC Document, 2009.

16. S. Chatterjee and M. D. Abkowitz, "A methodology for modeling regional terrorism risk," *Risk Analysis*, vol. 31, no. 7, pp. 1133–1140, 2011.

17. S. Kaplan and B. J. Garrick, "On the quantitative definition of risk," *Risk Analysis*, vol. 1, no. 1, pp. 11–27, 1981.

18. E. Pat-Cornell and S. Guikema, "Probabilistic modeling of terrorist threats: A systems analysis approach to setting priorities among countermeasures," *Military Operations Research*, vol. 7, no. 4, pp. 5–23, 2002.

19. G. D. Wyss, J. F. Clem, J. L. Darby, K. Dunphy-Guzman, J. P. Hinton, and K. W. Mitchiner, "Risk-based cost-benefit analysis for security assessment problems," in *Security Technology (ICCST), 2010 IEEE International Carnahan Conference*, pp. 286–295, IEEE, 2010.

20. T. Masse, S. O'Neil, and J. Rollins, "The Department of Homeland Security's risk assessment methodology: Evolution, issues, and options for Congress," DTIC Document, 2007.

21. Q. Li and D. Schaub, "Economic globalization and transnational terrorism a pooled time-series analysis," *Journal of Conflict Resolution*, vol. 48, no. 2, pp. 230–258, 2004.

22. A. Freytag, J. J. Krüger, D. Meierrieks, and F. Schneider, "The origins of terrorism: Cross-country estimates of socio-economic determinants of terrorism," *European Journal of Political Economy*, vol. 27, pp. S5–S16, 2011.

23. C. Carter, "Pre-incident indicators of terrorist attacks: Weak economies and fragile political infrastructures bring rise to terrorist organizations and global networks.," *Global Security Studies*, vol. 3, no. 4, 2012.

24. C. Street, "The origin of terror: Affluence, political freedom, and ideology," *An Empirical Study of the Risk Factors of International Terrorism*, 2008.

25. L. Elbakidze and Y. Jin, "Victim countries of transnational terrorism: An empirical characteristics analysis," *Risk analysis*, vol. 32, no. 12, pp. 2152–2165, 2012.

26. W. Enders, G. A. Hoover, and T. Sandler, "The changing nonlinear relationship between income and terrorism," *Journal of Conflict Resolution*, 2014.

27. J. A. Piazza, "Incubators of terror: Do failed and failing states promote transnational terrorism?," *International Studies Quarterly*, vol. 52, no. 3, pp. 469–488, 2008.

28. D. Kilcullen, *The accidental guerrilla: Fighting small wars in the midst of a big one.* Oxford University Press, 2009.

29. Q. Li, "Does democracy promote or reduce transnational terrorist incidents?," *Journal of Conflict Resolution*, vol. 49, no. 2, pp. 278–297, 2005.

30. K. Drakos and A. Gofas, "The devil you know but are afraid to face underreporting bias and its distorting effects on the study of terrorism," *Journal of Conflict Resolution*, vol. 50, no. 5, pp. 714–735, 2006.

31. W. W. Piegorsch, S. L. Cutter, and F. Hardisty, "Benchmark analysis for quantifying urban vulnerability to terrorist incidents," *Risk Analysis*, vol. 27, no. 5, pp. 1411–1425, 2007.

32. M. Feridun and S. Sezgin, "Regional underdevelopment and terrorism: the case of south eastern Turkey," *Defence and Peace Economics*, vol. 19, no. 3, pp. 225–233, 2008.

33. G. Khusrav, S. Todd, and S. Donggyu, "Common drivers of transnational terrorism: principal component analysis," *Economic Inquiry*, vol. 51, no. 1, pp. 707–721, 2013.

34. T. Krieger and D. Meierrieks, "What causes terrorism?," *Public Choice*, vol. 147, no. 1-2, pp. 3–27, 2011.

35. L. Schoenenberger, A. Schenker-Wicki, and M. Beck, "Analysing terrorism from a systems thinking perspective," *Perspectives on Terrorism*, vol. 8, no. 1, 2014.

36. J. A. Piazza, "Poverty, minority economic discrimination, and domestic terrorism," *Journal of Peace Research*, vol. 48, no. 3, pp. 339–353, 2011.

37. J. L. Geffre and D. E. Brown, "Quantitative framework for strategic spatial decisions," *Western Decision Sciences Conference Proceeding*, vol. 4, 3 2013.

38. J. Odenhal and J. M. Alek, "The determinants of terrorism risk–empirical analysis," *Recent Advances in Energy, Enviorment, and Economic Development*, vol. 3, pp. 286–291, 2012.

39. K. P. Burnham and D. R. Anderson, *Model selection and multimodel inference: a practical information-theoretic approach.* Springer Science & Business Media, 2002.

40. K. P. Burnham and D. R. Anderson, "Multimodel inference understanding AIC and BIC in model selection," *Sociological methods & research*, vol. 33, no. 2, pp. 261–304, 2004.

41. T. Hastie, R. Tibshirani, J. Friedman, T. Hastie, J. Friedman, and R. Tibshirani, *The elements of statistical learning*, vol. 2. Springer, 2009.

42. S. Arlot and A. Celisse, "A survey of cross-validation procedures for model selection," *Statistics surveys*, vol. 4, pp. 40–79, 2010.

43. Fund for Peace, "Fragile state index 2014." Fund for Peace, June 2014. http://library.fundforpeace.org/library/cfsir1423-fragilestatesindex2014-06d.pdf.

44. Ferdi, "LDC criteria." United Nations Development Policy and Analysis Division, October 2014.

45. J. Hilbe, *Negative binomial regression*. Cambridge University Press, 2011.